the HAWAIIAN HOUSE *now*

the HAWAIIAN HOUSE *now*

Photographs by Linny Morris

Text by Malia Mattoch McManus

with Jeanjean Bower

ABRAMS, NEW YORK

Editor: Charles Kochman
Designer: Susan Evans/Design per se
Production Manager: Jules Thomson

Library of Congress Cataloging-in-Publication Data

Mattoch McManus, Malia.
  The Hawaiian house now / photographs by Linny
  Morris ; text by Malia Mattoch McManus ; with
  Jeanjean Bower.
      p.cm
  ISBN-13: 978-0-8109-9394-5 (hardcover with
    jacket)
  ISBN-10: 0-8109-9394-5 (hardcover with jacket)
  1. Architecture, Domestic—Hawaii.
  2. Architecture—Hawaii—20th century.
  3. Architecture—Hawaii—21st century.
  I. Morris, Linny. II. Bower, Jeanjean. III. Title.

  NA7235.H3M38 2007
  728.09969—dc22

                              2007016340

Text copyright ©2007 Malia Mattoch McManus
Photographs copyright ©2007 Linny Morris

Published in 2007 by Abrams, an imprint of
Harry N. Abrams, Inc.

Printed and bound in China
10 9 8 7 6 5 4 3 2 1

HNA ■ ■ ■ ■ ■
harry n. abrams, inc.
a subsidiary of La Martinière Groupe

115 West 18th Street
New York, NY 10011
www.hnabooks.com

ACKNOWLEDGMENTS

The authors and photographer would
like to thank Hawaiian Airlines for
its support.

Debbie Brown and Geoffrey Bourne;
Jennica Brigham; Doug and Sharon
Britt; Jay Freis and Heeraa Sazevich;
Steve Kreider, Gretchen Fisher, Tessa
and Zena Kreider; the Kohl family
and the Chelseas; Michelle Lin; Dodie
and Doug MacArthur; Dug Miller;
Gail Miller and Raymond Miller Jr.;
William Neil; Pam Peterson; Christine
and Tim Thevenard; Roger Thorson;
Louli Yardley and Bill Guy; and most
of all, George Robertson.

                    —Linny Morris

Special thanks to Ian and Judy Mattoch,
the Kobayashi family, Jessica Dittrich,
Nate Smith, Florence Chong, Aubrey
Yee, Richard Olsen, Kevin Lake, Gina
Cook, Joanne Rixon, and Anne Oliver.

              —Malia Mattoch McManus

I would like to thank my parents for
their love and encouragement.

                    —Jeanjean Bower

DEDICATION

To my parents, Betty and Bill, who
together created our house in
Kaimalino, a timeless Hawaiian
original
—LM

To Jon and Jack, the highlights
of my home
—MMM

To John, Ty, Ellia, and Teke
—JJB

Page 2: Oʻahu resident Sue Bixler
commissioned artist David Diggs
to create this monstera, banana
leaf, and Tahitian gardenia pattern
on the arched living room ceiling
of her 1936 Kailua home. The
room's throw pillows are covered
in Tahitian pareo fabric.

CONTENTS

Ask an impassioned Hawai'i resident what their favorite thing about their home is, and it will likely be nothing material. It might be a certain view, or the experience of sitting on the *lānai* (porch) and listening to the movement of trees or the roll of waves. In Hawai'i, good design provides comfort, tells a story, and can sometimes set a spectacular stage, but it never tries to trump its setting. For native Hawaiians, the *mana*, or spirit, of the land is everything, and it is fitting that its power should continue to move us, regardless of how new or old our families are to the Islands.

A generation ago, Russian-born Vladimir Ossipoff designed a clean-lined structure in a grove of eucalyptus above Honolulu. It took him two years to decide how to do justice to the acre he built on, and when he did, he designed its core to allow the dweller to watch the forest light move across the space the entire length of the day. He curved the lines of a master bedroom rather than cut down a line of trees. That is a Hawaiian at heart.

When that Hawaiian voice is lost, the result is a structure more in tune with the setting of a city block, a place in which there is no shade, no fragrance. It could be picked up and transported to the desert and feel exactly the same. The twenty homes featured in this book would be vastly different experiences if moved, and not just if moved from Hawai'i.

Even a single mile would change these houses, because each design took into account the most dramatic view of the property. Each was built after studying how wind and light passed over the site. Some sit in the rain forest. Many are on the ocean. A few are high on a volcanic slope. All are surrounded by landscapes of such character that, if altered, the change would irrevocably impact the home.

Hawai'i gives any architect the opportunity to design with heightened awareness of the setting's light and air. Year-round temperate weather permits walls to slide open and breeze to flow through. Rooms extend seamlessly onto the lānai to create a living space where the lines between man's structure and nature's setting dissolve. Hawaii's light is so saturated with gold that any well-placed wall becomes memorably patterned with the sun's movement.

It is an opportunity that has attracted some of the world's best design talent. On Oahu's Kāhala beach, Aman Resorts architect Ed Tuttle created a structure with not a single solid exterior wall, allowing the entire house to open up and seemingly float. "I designed it for Hawai'i because the sense of architectural space here is easily and dramatically extended due to the idyllic climate," says Tuttle. "I like the tremendous advantage of being able to live in the open air basically year round, and the possibility of living amid nature."

Natural materials like coral, wood, lava stone, and *lauhala* matting (woven of the native hala tree), bring nature indoors as well as reminding the conscious dweller of the legacy of those who mastered the application of those elements. Native Hawaiians, New England missionaries, and the Asian families who initially immigrated to work Hawaii's sugar and pineapple plantations have all brought their style of living to the Islands. Their combined legacy is the foundation of what is authentic in current Hawai'i architecture.

When architect Don Vita set out criteria for the construction of an ambitious new Big Island development, he listed the need for historical authenticity and cohesiveness, but he also sought the use of traditional materials in a contemporary way. The same coral and lava rock that missionary families used to create some of Hawaii's most admired nineteenth- and early twentieth-century structures are now being used to construct the most modern of island homes.

Tuttle's design contains little reference to "traditional" Hawaiian architecture, yet it is fabricated out of white coral. Similarly, a contemporary Big Island home recently built into the slope of the slumbering Hualālai volcano was built out of the time-honored materials of wood and lava. While these new structures are architecturally a world away from their forbearers, they feel authentic. Their materials tie them to our history, and their openness to the environment ties them to the land.

Stewardship of the land was the final component on Vita's list, and it is on this point that Hawai'i design most often succeeds or fails. A burst of outside wealth in the 1980s unleashed a wave of construction built out to property lines and then sealed up and air-conditioned. It's an approach that most working architects see as an unfortunate waste of the Hawaiian setting.

"Closed-up buildings that use marble and dislocated architectural styles are a fast-food version of the Hawaiian experience," says Vita. "When authenticity is compromised, the result is a diluted or theme-park style interpretation that is stylized and lacking in substance."

"You're in Hawai'i for the air, the beauty of the breeze," says interior designer Michael S. Smith. "It's antithetical to live in a luxurious box. You want to have a sense of the place, the history, these interesting people who came together to form Hawaii's true style."

But if Hawaii's thriving economy and the influx of outside interest have pushed some unfortunate trends, they've also brought in top-tier talent—talent that is joining local voices in rediscovering what it takes to live well here: the use of cross-ventilation, natural materials, and a profound interaction with the surrounding environment.

"We've seen the mansions that treat the Hawaiian landscape as something to be seen from a climate-controlled treasure box rather than experienced through one's routine," says Honolulu architect Nate Smith. "On the other hand, thankfully, there's been a resurgence of interest in older homes that were sensitively designed and executed to reflect a quieter, slower time."

Homes that were at one time being scrapped are now being modified with modern luxuries, and classic styles are being reinterpreted into new construction. Local families are increasingly choosing classic Hawaiian plantation elements:

a sloped roof, the wrap-around lānai. Their great-grand parents may have lived in the same style on a working plantation, and a generation ago it was a style that might have seemed dated. But those elements work, and plantation architecture, with better kitchens and bigger living spaces, has reemerged as a younger person's choice.

That style is put to grander application in the Lanikai beach house featured in this book. With an ample lot and stunning views, the economics of this oceanfront estate and that of the traditional worker's plantation dwelling are vastly different, but the materials are exactly the same: board and batten walls, poured concrete floors, a shingle roof angled to keep sun off the windows. It's an architecture that has proved itself worthy against the Hawaiian test of sand, salt, and sun.

On a hill looking down on Lanikai Beach, a modern structure sits on a cliff built with walls of glass and fashioned in the tradition of Frank Lloyd Wright. At first glance we may ask, What makes that Hawaiian? A combination of the doors that open out to a deck that melts into native grass undulating in the same waves and blue-green tone of the sea below it, and the architect's choice to let hillside rock break through the walls and become part of the house rather than be shut off with a heavy layer of dry wall. The rock is part of a ridge named Ka Iwi on which native Hawaiians built sacred *heiau* (temples). Now a portion of it will always remind this home's dwellers where they live and how lucky they are to do so.

In up-country Maui, another family lives on the slope of Haleakalā in a house the owner's family built in the 1870s. Here the glass was cut by hand in unevenly shaped windows that look out onto wild roses and mountain ferns. But as in Lanikai, it is what lies outside the window that drives the life within. From Haleakalā, it's the view of mountain,

ocean, and the neighboring island of Lāna'i, a view unchanged in the four generations that have lived here. In Lanikai, it's the spotting of meteor showers and passing whales. On the slopes of Hualālai, it's living so high that clouds come through open walls.

On the Kona Coast, a landscape of seemingly barren, rugged lava that went relatively unnoticed for decades has been transformed to some of the most expensive land in the state because of the power of architecture. A luxury hotel that was originally planned as a high rise underwent a redesign that brought it down and sprinkled it along the ocean. Suddenly, the charm of a barefoot resort without elevators or massive concrete walls brought the emphasis on the setting: the flawless weather, the drama of black lava mixed with white sand and green naupaka. In came the private jets and an influx of luxury homebuilders unparalleled in Hawaii's history. But whereas twenty years ago they might have built pillared mansions, today many are falling in step with what it was that brought them to Hawai'i by building homes that open up to lava fields and ocean rather than marble fountains.

These are not houses that represent the realities of day-to-day living in Hawai'i, but they are recognizable as part of an island experience. We need only compare them to resort development of the 1980s to realize how far our current design vocabulary has come in evolving back to what works here.

"It's an exciting time," says Nate Smith. "Local and mainland talent are blending their residential ideas of past and present into a current solution, all of which ought to be evaluated on their respect for the land, climate, and culture and not some specific point in time."

Some of the new luxury development on the Big Island and elsewhere in Hawai'i has drawn the ire of architects for relying too heavily on the compatible solutions of Bali, Indonesia. We've covered this ongoing trend in this book because, when done well, the borrowing is an influence rather than merely a replication, and facets of this style are being absorbed into Island design.

Hawai'i has always been a benevolent meeting ground of cultures, and our own style roots come from the importation of what were once someone else's traditions. Compare the classic Hawaiian-style "Dickey" roof used in this book's Mokulē'ia property (page 60) to that of the new Balinese style roof at the Mākena residence (page 32). Both allow hot tropical air to rise to the top of the room and cool the home. Both angle out at the base to protect the home and its views. Both work well in Hawai'i, though the Dickey roof has a far longer history here.

The 1940s-era Mokulē'ia structure is wonderfully familiar to nearly every child in the Islands who grew up spending a weekend at someone's beach house: feet sandy, hair pasted wet to necks, stretched out on the *pune'e* (daybed) fighting off sleep while parents played cards with the radio on, their beers poured over ice harvested from the Styrofoam cooler just outside the screen door. The children pictured in the Mākena house have a plunge pool and top-of-the-line kitchen appliances, but the sliding doors of their home will be open to that same ocean sound that made it impossible for an earlier generation to keep their eyes open one second longer.

This collection of homes demonstrates where current Hawai'i design has succeeded and historic Hawai'i has remained relevant. Each incorporate some element of classic Hawaiian

interior design, whether in its art, rattan, or koa pieces, the Hawaiian quilt, or the beloved pune'e. But these personal spaces are also a wonderfully eclectic mix of comfortable Hawaiian style and new influences. They respect the past, but move onward rather than recycling what's always been done.

To go forward, it's helpful to go back to the beginning. The earliest Hawaiian structures were embedded with symbolic meanings and purposes that spanned birthing rituals to burial rites. Areas were created for the arrival of the young, a home's height often signified one's place in the community, and ancestors were sometimes buried within the stone platforms *hale* (houses) were built upon. "The structures themselves," says Nate Smith, "remained functional and wonderfully simple. They were done with spiritual thoughtfulness."

While living in Hawai'i has grown far more complicated and comfortable than those earliest times, that same thoughtfulness exists in the homes presented here. Despite the collective value of millions of dollars worth of building materials and furnishings represented in this book, not a single homeowner cited a possession or portion of their home's structure as their favorite part of their house. Instead they told stories of how they feel when afternoon light falls on their art. Or how the framing of a certain window draws their eyes toward a mountain no matter how hectic their day. Or the joy of smelling kāhili ginger from their bedroom and watching children surf from their kitchen. The owners' pleasures were different but held the same truth. Beyond function, it is the way these homes compel those living within them to be conscious of their setting that is today's measure of a Hawaiian house.

the new guard

THE KŪKIʻO COTTAGE

It was during an Oʻahu family vacation that Don Vita, then immersed in the planning of an incredibly luxurious Big Island resort community named Kūkiʻo, found his design inspiration in a humble beachside cottage.

"We were staying at Bellows Air Force Station, and although the cottage was tiny and spartan," says Vita, "it was located right on the sand, and the ease and casualness of it made it one of the best vacations ever. Casualness is the hallmark of the Hawaiian lifestyle. I think it is this relaxed atmosphere that draws people here."

Together with architect David Howerton, Vita created a series of structures connected by landscaped pathways, a design loosely based on the Indonesian "pod" system. The result is opulent in comparison with its original inspiration, but retains the carefree Hawaiian air Vita was so charmed by. Guests nap in their separate bedroom pavilions, meeting up barefoot on the garden paths connecting their rooms. The plunge pool doubles as a reflecting pond to palm trees and the light of a fire bowl. To swim, sleep, eat, or visit, one must walk by puakenikeni trees and banks of heliconia, and those short paths start to unwind the routine of car, door, office, car, and home that everyday life pushes upon us.

"The pavilion format certainly lends itself well to resort living, since it is relaxed, even playful," says Howerton.

Kūkiʻo at dusk. The Indonesian compound concept was reinterpreted with high-end design, electronics, and appliances, as well as an awareness of the Hawaiian volcanic setting. Building insulation prevents the copper roof from heating up the home.

The cottage's lava rock and ʻōhiʻa wood entrance. ʻŌhiʻa was traditionally used by Hawaiians for poi boards, canoe construction, and as the enclosure around temples. Today it's a highly desired material for flooring as well as posts, due to its distinctive sinuous branches.

As romantic as the experience is, Vita says the design is quite practical for a vacation home. "It allows for the separation of the public and private functions, creating open spaces for the living areas and privacy for the bedroom or guest quarters."

Howerton sees the outdoor spaces as a part of the home's design. "It's a way of building and landscaping that utilizes the tropical climate to create homes that are effortlessly connected to the natural environment."

The lānai and plunge pool extend off the living room so seamlessly it feels the space stops only at the volcanic anchialine pond below. The ponds are central to Kūkio's design and the source of the area's name. *Kūki'o* is Hawaiian for standing ponds, or pools of water. Ocean and lava fields complete the landscape. Kūkio's planners integrated this vibrant living space into the home's view and used them as inspiration for structural materials, insisting that the building palette not compete with the natural setting.

A plunge pool just off the living room fronts one of Kūkio's anchialine ponds. As well as rehabilitating and restocking the property's historic ponds, which had become degraded with invasive, non-native species, the developer created new ponds indistinguishable from the natural ponds, stocking them with native 'ōpae'ula shrimp and fish.

Stone and wood form the base of the cottage construction, along with a copper roof that by natural oxidation will be rendered a green that subordinates to the landscape. "Its natural color recedes rather than advances to the viewer," says Howardton, who notes that copper is also long-lasting in the punishing ocean trade winds.

Interior designer Jon Staub used color-saturated fabrics and wall treatments to balance out the neutral tones of the building materials. "The home is beautiful and very woody. If you'd put neutral tones on top of it, the whole thing would just blend out. There's such simulation here between the interiors and the exterior setting that you want to bring those greens and blues and garden reds inside."

Imperial plaster walls, *pūne'e* (daybeds) covered in beautifully woven French fabrics: the pleasures of Kūki'o are rich and yet subtle. There is no marble, no grand entry. The entrance is an 'ōhi'a wood gate wonderfully overgrown with vine. It takes just long enough to open, that you catch the sun-drenched scent of flowering trees on both sides. The effect is one of anticipation and the slightest touch of drowsiness.

"It's all about resort living," says Staub. "Instead of sitting upright in your seat, you're slightly slouched, perfectly happy and almost about to fall asleep. That's how this home feels."

Huge cedar timber ceiling beams throughout the cottage are structural. Doors in the same cedar wood open onto garden pathways. Blue imperial plaster gives the living room a backdrop of color, and a bowl of lavender-hued *wana* (sea urchin) shells bring a reminder of the ocean nearby.

Honeycomb ginger from the Hilo side of the Big Island join French-made textiles that interior designer Jon Staub of Philpotts and Associates chose for the living room as a stepped-up version of the traditional Hawaiian bark cloth.

The rich materials of the master bath are matched by the luxury of a private garden outside. The very narrow exterior space provides color and an outdoor shower.

The master bedroom backboard reminded Jon Staub of Kona's kiawe trees: "I also wanted to work with the ʻōhiʻa fence surrounding this bedroom and bring it indoors." Through the sliding doors, the master lānai connects the room to the spa.

In the guest bedroom, monstera leaf-patterned bedspreads in soft linen provide the high contrast Staub wanted between wood and color-saturated prints.

The guest room desk enjoys a view into heliconia-filled gardens and a print by renowned island artist Jean Charlot. Cedar flooring is used in all the bedrooms.

Fronted by a red-blossomed coral tree, the cottage spa reflects the ʻōhiʻa fencing used throughout the property. Beyond the spa lie coconut trees, lava, and an anchialine pond.

Well-designed landscape and ʻōhiʻa post fencing create both a privacy buffer outside the master bathroom, as well as an outdoor shower area. "Because the cottages are laid out compactly," says Howerton, "the biggest challenge was how to ensure privacy."

On the mauka lānai, an Australian clamshell rests atop a lacquered wooden pillar. The Chinese urn holding the bromeliad is an early Ching Dynasty granite jardinere.
The house's stucco work is a nod to the owners' love of the Honolulu Academy of Arts and was done in the same off-white tone of the Academy's walls.

Honolulu architect John Hara has designed major contemporary additions to such venerated Hawai'i landmarks as the historic Punahou School and the Honolulu Academy of Arts. His work is marked by a commitment to Hawaiian architectural tradition and the desire to push that tradition forward.

"We need to respect Hawai'i design without freezing it in time," says Hara, who successfully struck that balance at this oceanfront residence on the Big Island.

Designed as a family compound, Hara created three different buildings rather than one enormous house for the owners, Don and Sally Lucas, who are admirers and patrons of the Honolulu Academy of Arts.

The Academy's 1920s design by Bertram Goodhue and Hardie Phillip is frequently cited as an inspiration to architects, and this structure's off-white plaster work, pillars, and generous lānai are highly reminiscent of the Academy's style. But Hara cautions that the house is not a version of the museum. "It's a contemporary use of the classic, old Hawaiian plaster style for its own reasons. The plaster shows off art well and accentuates interior light."

Modern expectations of good natural light throughout the house led Hara to add rows of skylights wherever the three dwellings' roofs met. That placement was the answer to the area's guidelines requiring sloped rather than flat roofs. While the shingle roof is one any early twentieth century Hawai'i architect would recognize, the skylights are a twist none of them would have made.

"This is a deep house, and the skylights introduced natural light in a necessary way that people couldn't do in the 1920s and '30s," says Hara. "It wasn't part of the aesthetic then, but it is now, and it can be done in a way that doesn't obscure what is traditional about the home. That balance is part of what I've tried to do for many years."

Hara has also tried to revive building traditions that have become rare. The plaster work done at the Academy is known for its "lumpy" texture, but modern plaster work is rarely anything but smooth. The materials used under the plaster have changed. In the 1920s, plaster was applied over lava rock, giving it a bumpy surface. But lava is far too precious to employ in the same way today, and plasterers have become accustomed to producing utterly smooth work over the flatness of cement block.

"I joked with the owners that we needed to get the least experienced plaster worker we could so that they wouldn't make it too perfect," says Hara with a smile. "Actually, reviving this style is a very fine skill. You need to lay the plaster unevenly to create the bump. That's difficult, but it worked here."

The kitchen was designed in a way so that no views were blocked from the entry of the house to the ocean. Italian cocciopesto countertops were paired with integral concrete floors done in nearly the same green shade by craftsman Mark Lesnick. Rosalie Prussing paintings of various island scenes hang on the right. A painting of the Big Island coast by Guy Lam, the house's contractor, hangs on the left.

This home also gave Hara the opportunity to incorporate the stained-concrete floors that were once ever-present in classic Hawai'i design.

"I've wanted to do those for years, but a lot of the knowledge of how to do it properly died with the men who were pouring those floors in the 1940s. Nowadays it's more painterlylike," says Hara. "But the owners wanted to produce that feel. The concrete floors recall part of Hawaii's history. They were intent to reflect that and the informal lifestyle of beach living: the natural ventilations and the mauka and makai lānai."

Sally Lucas, who acted as interior designer, found the answer in Californian concrete artist Mark Lesnick, who produced the right texture and shade of green for the floors. Lucas wanted the home's classic Hawaiian palette of green and white to be energized with her favorite tones of orange and reds, choosing pieces that were comfortable and easy on the family and guests.

"This home is Hawaiian in that it's welcoming, friendly, and easy, with an open-air lifestyle," says Lucas, who agrees with Hara that at its heart it is still essentially a beach house.

In the master bathroom,
the bath and shower open to
a garden of plumeria, pīkake,
gardenia, and monstera.

In the family room, chairs in Lucas's trademark colors are paired with an oil painting by Hawai'i artist Winifred Hudson. The painting was previously on loan to Honolulu's Contemporary Art Museum.

In the dining room, a handmade brass table by Los Angeles artist Christian Heckscher. Behind the table, an antique Japanese screen bought by the owners in Kyoto and a hand-carved fish found on a trip in Italy. On the left, an antique Chinese armoire.

"We designed a wood ceiling for it, but it would have been too much," says Hara. "It's not as finished as what we would do for a house people live in full time. It's a gracious house and a comfortable one. It has an informal elegance and retains that old Hawai'i spirit while still feeling modern. It's a simple house. One might consider that a design challenge. In the end, you work very hard to make it simple."

When the Lucas family first bought the land, views of the beach were almost entirely blocked by kiawe trees, which were cleared and replaced with coconut palms. The lap pool was done in gray plaster and glass tile.

On the lawn, a ceramic sculpture by artist Jun Kaneko. The owners met him while they were building an artist residence center in Saratoga, California. Kaneko maintains a home and studio on the island of Kaua'i.

A perfectly shaped Chinese banyan tree and Jorg Madlener's painting *Equus* greet visitors at the home's elegant entry.

The building is done entirely in concrete and steel, opening up to both the mauka and makai lānai.

The architecture of Bali, Indonesia, solves many of the same issues Hawaiian architecture addresses: airflow in a humid environment, sporadic but heavy downpours of rain, and the integration of stunning natural surroundings. It's no surprise then that many Hawai'i homeowners have taken a page out of a Balinese design book and made it their own.

"It's made a huge impact on Hawaiian design in recent years, and well-designed versions of what I call 'Polynesian-Balinesian' style work very well here," says Jim Niess, a Maui architect who designed Paul Moreno and Bruce Gilpin's Mākena home, one of the better examples of this island trend.

The home is located on a narrow stretch of ocean view property. When Moreno and Gilpin first saw the property, it was initially difficult to appreciate its potential. "It sort of looked like a garbage dump," says Moreno. In fact, the site had been used as a dumping area for clean, excavated fill from the construction of the Maui Prince Hotel. Once Moreno and Gilpin climbed up to the top of the property, they saw that the views of the ocean and offshore islands were incredible, and their design process began.

"We had seen so many homes that seemed out of place in Maui that we were inspired to build a tropical house," says Moreno.

The shallow, three-quarter acre lot presented initial design challenges, as did the placement of a mature kiawe tree the owners did not want to remove. Landscaper William Neil chose large planting blocks of dwarf croton and iris philodendron for dramatic color and texture, and incorporated native plants that would flourish in Mākena's dry microclimate.

"Our home is not the typical Wailea-style home that you see in this part of Maui. It's not hermetically sealed with air-conditioning and marble floors, nor is it multi-story."

Instead, Moreno and Gilpin had Niess design a structure which blends subtropical architectures: a high-pitched roof, natural materials, and general openness to the environment, with the luxury features popular in a twenty-first century structure: an open plan layout, extensive kitchen intended as a social center, and an extreme consciousness of views.

"The home's slide-away walls with continuous flooring materials help blur the distinction between interior and exterior and bring attention to the setting," says Niess, who notes that it is also one of several choices the owners made to avoid the need to seal themselves up in air-conditioning due to Mākena's hot, dry weather. The building's relatively narrow rooms amplify the breezeway effect of cross-ventilation. The distinctive high-volume roof draws heat away from its residents.

"The exposed roof framing also provides historical and cultural reference to the earliest Hawaiian structures," says Niess, referencing the indigenous Hawaiian hale using an exposed-beam thatched roof.

Radiating, exposed Brazilian cherry wood beams mark the dramatic ceiling. "They remind me of the solid ribs of an old sailing vessel," says William Neil. Maui designer Persis Hataria had the woven bamboo matting installed on the ceiling for greater dimension.

Indonesian Palimanan stone flooring runs continuously between the indoor and outdoor space. An eleven-foot slab of teak serves as the dining room table, while in the background stands a contemporary version of the traditional Hawaiian koa buffet.

The pool offers views of Kahoʻolawe and the crescent-shaped islet of Molokini. The owners wanted a lap pool with a negative edge spilling away from the house that could be lit for drama.

Niess draws the comparison between this roof and the classic Hawaiian Dickey roof, a steep, double-pitched roofline popularized by architect Charles W. Dickey that provided air flow to the home's interior and then gracefully spread out to provide shade and rain protection to the structure's walls.

While the results are by no means traditional Hawaiian architecture, the finest elements of this trend are time-tested aspects of tropical design that Niess believes fulfill the vision of a sustainable architecture appropriate to twenty-first century Hawai'i.

"We need to employ design that responds to its setting without dominating it," says Niess. "Design that brings back the comfort of natural materials and organic spaces, which lays light on the land and can be recycled for another generation's inspiration."

A dramatic brushed-stainless steel tub fills a niche built out of the master bathroom. Pebble tile was used around the base to give it visual reference to the nearby ocean. One can rinse the salt and sand off on the deck outside before stepping directly into the generously sized shower.

Imperial plaster bedroom walls impart a feeling of coolness in the sometimes wilting heat of Mākena. Next to the lamp sits a bronze sculpture that landscaper William Neil cast from a seed pod. The owners installed air-conditioning in the bedroom and kitchen for rare scorching days, but rely mostly on cross-ventilation.

The double-pitched roof respects both Asian and Hawaiian architectural tradition. While the roof was designed before breaking ground, much of the structure's design work was done during the course of construction, allowing for a greater degree of customization.

Mākena at sunset with a view of neighboring Lānaʻi. This area of Maui was traditionally known for its fishing and rocky shoreline beauty. The "green flash" islanders wait to see at sunset along the horizon is a frequent scene on this shoreline.

The large wood pocket doors use a floor tracking system in which the space between each track is tiled. The threshold between indoor and outside is unnoticeable.

"We built this home so that it would almost disappear," says design/build contractor Gregg Todd of the Big Island residence of Toni and KC Knudson. "We tried to minimize the building to subtly blend with its surroundings. The home became a backdrop for the planting rather than a bold architectural statement."

With mammoth pocket doors that allow walls to slide away and a courtyard entrance that draws the eye straight through the pavilion-style living room out to the ocean, Todd's design succeeds in bringing the visitor past the structure, letting them focus instead on the tremendous views and art collection of the home.

Both the home's setting and its historic Hawaiian art reflect the Knudsons' taste for classic Hawai'i. Museum-quality pieces by major Island artists Lionel Walden, David Howard Hitchcock, Hubert Vos, and Joseph Sharp hang in every room of their otherwise low-key interiors.

"Living in Hawai'i, I try to avoid being overdone or too formal," says Toni Knudson, who began collecting Hawaiian regional art with her husband KC while they were in construction with their first home in the Islands. "I think it's important to represent local artists and reflect the culture in your home."

Walden's 1908 *Crashing Waves* is the focal point of a living room which Toni and interior design partner Gina Willman finished in neutral tones to allow the art to stand out. The actual ocean scene beyond the room's invisible walls was given similar consideration by Gregg Todd. "We framed the home's view of the ocean by positioning the pool so that your eye would move from the grass of the lawn over the break of water and then down the green of the resort out to the ocean," says Todd. "That layering of color gives the ocean an even greater impact."

Another strategic treatment of exterior space lies outside the master bedroom. "Outdoor showering has become almost a pre-requisite in resort communities here," says Willman. "We really did not have the exterior space to incorporate the outdoor shower, so we placed the shower and bath adjacent to the sliding doors. When the doors slide away you have the sense of being outdoors."

In the living room, a heart-stopping sight for any Hawai'i regional art collector, Lionel Walden's 1908 *Crashing Waves*. Walden has been called the finest seascape painter to work in Hawai'i. The Knudsons use this room and the exterior spaces it opens onto for private piano concerts in their home.

In the office, KC Knudson's personal collection of Joseph Sharp's Windward O'ahu landscapes. Toni Knudson and Gina Willman kept the room's finishes and furniture dark so that "the paintings' colors would just pop off the wall."

In one of the guest bedrooms, Cornelia Foley etchings hang above a bed with an Asian flavor in sumptuous fabrics by Clarence House. The walls were given a striae faux finish by Joe Eby to give this elegant room additional texture.

43

Todd notes that an outdoor shower also requires a lot of hardscape: the stepping stones to reach it and the shower pad. By bringing the shower back indoors, the garden became more lush.

"The whole bathroom is very subtle," says Willman. "We curved the shower wall to give the psychological feeling of it being a bit more enclosed." The addition of a custom-built six-foot-long molded concrete bathtub finishes the space with a sculptural touch. "The overall effect is simple but sensual," adds Willman.

In the entry courtyard, another romantic touch was established through the purchase of an Archie Held sculpture titled *Lovers*.

"Once the Knudsons chose the sculpture, the idea of lovers became our underlying theme for the area," says Willman. "So we commissioned a stone carving in the same vein, as well as a bronze bench for a couple to enjoy the sculptures."

"That courtyard is like having a living room outdoors," says Todd, who notes that the Knudsons chose stucco for the exterior walls specifically as a neutral backdrop to the surrounding sculptures and landscape. "It's a 'room' you want to linger in, and it's like the house. You start to forget whether you're inside or out."

The panoramic pool was angled on the lot to draw the eye to the best ocean view.

45

In the dining room, an 1898 portrait by Hubert Vos titled *Iokepa, Hawaiian Fisher Boy*. The Dutch-born Vos ventured to Hawai'i after meeting the beautiful, part-Hawaiian Eleanor Graham, who was traveling in the United States as a companion to Hawaii's Queen Lili'uokalani. The dining and living room rugs were commissioned by New Mexico-artist Joan Weissman.

The master bath opens out to a bamboo and river rock garden with a lava rock backdrop. The concrete bathtub's porous material necessitates a six-month maintenance schedule of beeswax finishing. A travertine-clad pillar conceals the plumbing intricacies and allows the water to spill in a sheet, filling the sculptural bathtub.

blue horizon—
green flash

This 1950s-era house was built on what had been the site of a fishing cottage. Momsen sought to revert it to a 1930s feel. From the lānai, the Momsens have views of Puakō's dolphin- and sea turtle-filled waters.

"It looked like a double-wide trailer when we bought it," says Carol Momsen of the Puakō beach house that is now her Big Island home. "Our friends from the mainland said, 'You're tearing it down, right? What are you going to build?'"

Instead, Momsen set out to rehabilitate a structure that had little in the way of charm.

"The pillars and posts that the house sat on were all exposed. It looked like someone had backed in the trailer and then walked away," says Momsen. After immediately putting lattice around the home's base, the Momsens began landscaping and added a porch and pitched roof to give the residence a proper entry.

"There were even things like exposed vent pipes in the middle of the kitchen," says Momsen, "but this was Hawai'i, so I could enclose the ugly pipe in a bamboo pole that became a theme in that part of the house."

Just as the building started to come around, the property next door became available. Carol and her husband Bob purchased it as a guest cottage and began the same mission to renovate rather than tear down.

By adding a trellis and lānai, Momsen revamped an adjoining 1960s cottage, which she described as having "architectural details I don't believe an architect had anything to do with. I wanted to transform it into the traditional green Hawaiian cottage."

A single mango sits atop the kitchen table covered in Momsen's favorite color combinations.

"Both the bedroom and kitchen in the cottage had linoleum that needed to go. I replaced it with the black and white vinyl tile, which is classic for the 1930s era." The green poured-cement floors are original to the house. "The lauhala mats cover them very strategically as certain areas did not hold up well."

Momsen's watercolors from a trip to Tahiti hang above a daybed inspired by a photograph of a striped pune'e from the 1930s. Pillows are done in contrasting bark cloth.

Puakō's famously clear water and lava rock pools are just beyond Momsen's property. Puakō was an important seaside area for ancient Hawaiians. They left nearly three thousand petroglyphs etched into the lava rock of the immediate area.

Once again they added a lānai to the home's front to create the entry it lacked and the island feel they'd envisioned. They removed the aluminum siding and replaced the original board and batten. And as she had in their main house, Momsen used trellising to trick the eye and create a break from the constant sunshine of the Kona coast.

"Trellising hides a multitude of sins. Both our house and cottage had architectural details that weren't beautiful. The cottage had a bad addition which the trellis instantly made invisible."

Though the cottage was built in the 1950s, and the main residence was done in the 1960s, Momsen gave both the feel of the 1930s, which she considers the most gracious era of the Hawaiian beach house. "We wanted to turn both of these very generic buildings into the classic Hawaiian cottages, and it worked. There's not much you have to knock down in Hawai'i if you add a lanai, some trellises, and clever landscaping. Now when my friends come back to stay, the ones who wanted us to build something new, they're wonderfully surprised."

A Hawaiian quilt given to the Momsens hangs in the cottage living room, attached with carpet tack. The furniture, from Plantation Interiors in Kona, was done in custom covers with contrasting welts to reflect Momsen's taste for the color combination of red and yellow.

55

A white thumbergia vine grows over Momsen's garden trellis. "There's greater flexibility with what you can do with a trellis than a wall," notes Momsen.

Antique Hawaiian feather lei are displayed in koa boxes crafted by neighbor and renowned koa woodworker John Martin. Highly sought-after koa wood, which grows only in Hawai'i and is used extensively for heirloom furniture, was traditionally used by Hawaiians for canoes and paddles, though not for food bowls, as it was thought to impart an unpleasant flavor.

Momsen's preferred setting for dinner. The table sits atop one of her collection of lauhala mats which the Kona area is known for.

Using bamboo poles, Momsen was able to hide exposed vent pipes in the kitchen. She painted the kitchen island black and then secured bamboo fencing over it to hide what she considered a dated-looking kitchen. "I tried to turn it into something beachy and natural." A collection of shell, kukui, and ti leaf lei hang from a dining room chair.

"Blue's not my favorite color," says Carol Momsen. "But since it's everyone else's and this is a guest cottage, I decided to do a blue room." The lamp is a vase from Chinatown that Momson wired. The bench was left in the yard by the former owner. Momsen had it painted red with an overlay of white.

Momsen added landscaping, a lānai with railings, and a false roof to soften the look of the home. The hale papa kea door was inspired by a similar detail at an old Oʻahu beach estate.

BEACH ART

Located literally at the end of a road, the area of Mokulē'ia on Oahu's North Shore retains an air of quieter times. Long established as a ranching community, this beach neighborhood hosts both country polo matches and quiet camping weekends for those wanting a respite from city living or the frenetic energy of nearby Hale'iwa during winter's big wave season. Mokulēia's extensive offshore reefs shelter swimmers from massive ocean swells and keep its surf spots primarily local.

"My brother and I came out to Mokulē'ia because our boys surfed out here. We fell in love with the house," says the owner of this classic Hawaiian beach home. "It had the feeling of living in a bit of old-time Hawai'i."

Built in the early 1940s, the structure survived the 1946 tidal wave with little damage while nearly every other house along Mokulēia's shoreline was virtually destroyed. In its early days, the house was owned by Hawaii's State Attorney General. "And rumor has it," says the current owner, "there were many parties held here by the Bar Association."

It's easy to see why: set on an acre of land, the residence has an overwhelming sense of privacy. It once functioned as a bed and breakfast until the owner tired of doing airport runs and decided to sell. The current owner removed fixed plate-glass windows and planted over a hundred coconut trees and more than two dozen large shade trees on the property, which had been empty and hot.

Two ceramic figures by sculptor Nina Kajiwara flank the front door. "We brought them out here to 'guard' the house," say the owners.

A coconut doll from the early twentieth century (when there was a strong visitor market for such products) sits on a hand-painted game table. All of the Hawaiiana in the house are pieces the owners have collected and reupholstered or refinished.

A collection of hibiscus paintings the owners have collected for years. "We like the various ways our state flower is depicted, depending on the artist," say the owners. Among the artists: Tip Freeman, Ted Mundorff, and Hale Pua, each of whom have several works represented here.

"We wanted something that took advantage of the breeze and was simply built, with airy rooms that opened to the grounds. We added outdoor showers. The pleasures here are straightforward."

The cottage furnishings are a throwback to vintage Hawaiiana: furniture from the 1950s and '60s as well as accent pieces from the early part of the twentieth century. It's a marked contrast to the couple's town house, which is thoroughly contemporary. "The Hawaiiana theme is particular to the Mokulē'ia house because it is an old-style house and we live that way when we're out there. The family weddings and parties held here have that same vintage feel."

"We wanted a utilitarian, comfortable place where family could sleep over and hang out in an environment that spoke of this particular part of the world and its uniqueness," say the owners, who filled this room of their beach house with pune'e. These beloved Hawaiian day beds are descended from the original Hawaiian hikie'e, fashioned of stacked woven lauhala mats. The metal sculpture in the window is by California artist Bulwinkle. "He uses a blow torch the way most artists use a paintbrush," say the owners. The bronze piece titled *Hare* is by Ken Little, a Texas artist.

The guest cottage is a play on tapa patterns. In addition to being an ancient Hawaiian art form, the traditional Polynesian designs were very popular in Hawai'i in the 1960s. The lampshades were painted by the owner. The wood block prints are by Hawai'i artist Dietrich Varez.

Less vintage is the couple's eclectic contemporary art collection, a delightful surprise in such a low-key beach home. John Buck and Deborah Butterfield sculptures greet visitors on the lawn. Nina Kajiwara pieces frame the front door. A Roy DeForest sculpture stands at one side of the living room, and a John Nava painting hangs over a piano. Their collection of major contemporary American artists seems especially charming placed amid the beach-worn furniture and they make this home feel dramatically different than the standard beach-rental look prevalent on the North Shore.

Many of the artists represented in the collection have stayed on the property at the couple's invitation. "I always thought the cottage would be a great studio," says the owner. "But it doesn't seem to be a place where you want to buckle down and work. It is a reminder of gentler times when people were not in such a rush. Time slows down here: getting in the ocean, walking on the beach. It's a wonderful place to pretend you have nothing else to do."

The classic Hawai'i beach house, with a double-slope roof that islanders call the "Dickey Roof." While the architect Charles W. Dickey did not design this home, he did influence this style of high-pitched roof that allowed for cooling air flow. It also angles outward at the bottom to protect exterior windows and walls from the sun's glare. To the right, the property's guest cottage, which is fronted by a Roy Deforest sculpture.

A young visitor sprints for the beach that lies just beyond the hedge on a path lined with a few of the home's 130 coconut trees. The aluminum band tacked around each trunk is commonly used in Hawai'i to prevent rats from nesting in the treetops.

An attractive and practical placement of river rock along the structure's exterior protects it from water damage and ground erosion, eliminating the need for a gutter system.

Gail Miller's favorite spot in the house: a generous lānai she added. She designed the lānai's chairs after being inspired by a photograph of furniture in her grandmother's 1921 University of Hawai'i yearbook.

In Miller's son's bedroom, an original oil on vellum painting by artist Carol Bennet of famed Hawaiian waterman, Duke Kahanamoku. The hala hats were done by master weaver Lynn Ham Young from Hā'ena. The bed is teak from Miller's furniture line.

THE KEKAHA PLANTATION HOUSE

"Hawai'i still lives in Kekaha," says Gail Miller of the sleepy West Kaua'i town she has lived in since 1999. "Children play their ukulele on the way to school. On a morning walk you may startle a pet pig that quickly runs for cover under the house. Hawaiian is freely spoken in the grocery store, sounding more like music than a language."

Where once a steam train delivered Kekaha's mail and carted off its sugar cane, this former plantation town is now reached by a single-lane road passing miles of white sand beach. Surfers and tourists line the shore to watch the sun drop into the western horizon at an hour that used to bustle with workers returning from the fields to their plantation homes.

Originally the plantation owners' humble answer to housing their labor force, the "plantation house" has taken on an iconic status in Hawai'i architecture. Deluxe remodels in the state's priciest suburbs seek to imbue multi-million dollar homes with elements of old plantation charm: single-wall board and batten construction; the steeply pitched roof originally used to cool rooms on a hot day; a front lānai that allowed working families an entertaining space on Sundays. These elements have been copied and romanticized by residents eager for a taste of "old" Hawai'i.

That authentic plantation homes have survived decades after sugar's demise is a testament to their suitability to island living and their owners' determination to keep the architectural tradition alive. When Gail Miller first saw this beachside plantation structure, it was badly in need of repair, with extensive termite damage and a ruined electrical system. But Miller could not resist the fact that much of the interior was in its original state.

"The wonderful old double-hung windows with the slight wave in the glass," says Miller. "The Douglas fir floors with the familiar squeak. And despite two hurricanes, the old canec ceilings were intact because of Kekaha's dry weather."

Built in 1931 by Kekaha Sugar Plantation for one of its supervisors, Miller's residence is both an authentic and highly glamorized example of the plantation style. While workers in the 1930s lived in cramped quarters, supervisors were given eminently more comfortable conditions.

"The house was built for entertaining, with a large butler's pantry housing a collection of cups for tea, and many *kama'āina* (longtime residents) remembering sipping tea on the porch."

Other than repairing the structure's damage and adding the lānai, Miller left it untouched. "There's still a hole in the rafters where two brothers once accidentally shot off a gun and quickly fabricated a story to their father about finding a rat in the attic and stepping through the ceiling. And to the old-timers, my guest quarters out back will always be

The oceanside front of Miller's home. The windows and doors on the front lānai are all original. The siding on the house was replaced due to termite damage. The upstairs lānai was added on to allow Miller to enjoy a view of the neighboring island of Ni'ihau.

The main home's dining room. The dining and side tables are made entirely of recycled materials and finishes. As an interior designer, Miller chose a neutral palate "to just relax and not be thinking about much color."

where a man named Hong Men Hee had a giant wok set up because he loved to cook and his wife did not want him messing up the kitchen."

Miller, an interior decorator, chose neutral interiors to highlight the beauty of the outdoor ocean setting as well as her own collection of memories: vintage koa canoe paddles, a grandmother's hula skirt from the 1930s, and menu covers from transpacific Matson Line voyages.

"I wanted my son to have a sense of where his family had come from. They were from the Big Island, Oʻahu, and Maui, not Kekaha or even Kauaʻi. But being in this house, you understand what it was like to live in the Hawaiʻi his great-grandparents knew. It's just gracious and very relaxing with the sound of the waves pounding away, lulling you to sleep with the perfume of plumeria wafting in the window."

A koa canoe paddle collection chosen by renowned Kauaʻi waterman Bobo Ham Young and an original Carol Bennett oil on vellum.

In the guest room, menu covers from a Californian great-grandmother's transpacific Matson Line voyages to Hawaiʻi.

The kitchen's layout is original to the home, with its classic black and white vinyl tiles requiring the old-fashioned maintenance of waxing.

The airy butler's pantry was a luxurious touch accorded only plantation management and owners.

Miller's television room. All of the furniture was custom-made for her design collection. The canec ceilings, fabricated from sugar cane and a common element of Hawai'i homes of this time period, are original.

The guest house as seen from the back lānai. The plumbing, electrical work, siding, as well as tongue and groove interiors all were redone by Miller.

In the foreground, the guest house roof of corrugated tin is a typical plantation touch, and a sentimental material for Island residents who grew up hearing its distinctive sound on a rainy night.

74

On a breezy day, Lanikai's Mokulua Drive is dusted with sand and busy with barefoot beachgoers. This pocket of O'ahu has remained noncommercial and retains some of the island's finest examples of Hawaiian beach house architecture. When architect Nancy Peacock took on the renovation of a 1929 bungalow here, she was adamant that she would restore the home to its original glory.

"We've tended to marginalize the fabulous skills and materials of the 1920s," Peacock says. "You just don't see that use of materials and construction techniques anymore. This home sits amid punishing conditions of wind and salt, yet it has survived so well. It was an epic building period in Hawai'i. Bar none, every one of them is a beauty."

The only Lanikai beach house listed on the State and National Register of Historic Places, the structure had undergone what Peacock describes as some "unfortunate" renovations over the years, including a badly conceived galley kitchen. It took two full years of design and construction to recapture some of the home's best original details and add a few modern conveniences.

A quiet corner on the original home's mauka (mountainside) lānai. This lānai is used on days of strong onshore ocean winds when the building acts as a shield to the courtyard. The wall is an intact original wall that captures the elegance and wonderfully textural quality of board and batten construction. The concrete floor was left a natural tone because the green stain used elsewhere on the property does not weather well when exposed to water.

Well-known designer Michael S. Smith selected a vintage bamboo children's game table and stools covered in Hawaiian bark cloth for this corner of the living room.

This venerable sea grape is the character tree of the yard, pruned to a height that provides the home privacy. The owners wanted a sustainable landscape: primarily native plants that did not require pesticides, which are used nowhere on the property. "As long as you pick the right plants and don't let it get out of control, you don't need pesticides," says Bornhorst.

Privacy concerns led the owners to use mature plants as privacy screens, including this hedge of naupaka and native grasses. "We've encouraged pōhuehue and nanea grasses to grow," says Bornhorst, "letting native Hawaiian shearwaters nest in a hedge of native grass."

The guest cottage in the foreground was new construction integrated with the pattern of the original house in the background through matched pillars. Peacock designed the grill work on the guest house as a more modern detail employed to bring down the scale of the covered walkway. The lawn is what landscaper Heidi Bornhorst calls "Hawaiian mix. There's some Harrington, el toro, Korean temple grass, and even some St. Augustine left from the thirties."

"It was complicated by the fact that this was on the Historic Register. I normally don't mess with that. But the clients needed a better kitchen. We also created a master bedroom from what had been an open lānai that someone had enclosed into a dark and airless room. I did not want the house to suffer from how I built this new wing."

Peacock matched the new wing's walls to the structure's existing board and batten, using similar spacing and pattern. She introduced stained concrete flooring to the new wing and portions of the old to unify the structure. The extraordinary copper patina green flooring is historically accurate to beach homes of the 1920s, as are the awning windows Peacock created to replace the fixed glass an intervening owner had installed.

"It's horrible to close up a house on the ocean," she says. "The original construction took tremendous consideration of cross-ventilation as they didn't have air conditioning."

"There was a good reason things used to be the way they were," says Honolulu landscaper Heidi Bornhorst, who wanted to bring the same element of classic Hawai'i to the property's grounds. "There used to be sand dunes all along this beach. They've all been harvested to make cement. When we dug out the pool, I told the contractor not to touch that sand, and I used it to recreate a dune in front of the house. This whole beach is eroding, but the sand in front of this house has been retained like nowhere else because of that dune."

Sand and salt air being a constant in this home, interior designer Michael S. Smith wanted to create "a kind of sparseness in the furnishings so that those things would work with the beach. I tried to buy things that were really evocative of a certain feeling but not so fine that it was a problem if they got damaged."

Pairing bamboo, wood, and rattan furniture with matchstick blinds, Chinese antiques, and a few vintage pieces from Hawaii, Smith echoed Peacock and Bornhorst's affinity for the past.

"I wanted to fill this home with the kind of things that are inherently Hawaiian from the golden age of the 1930s to the 1950s. I love that kind of kama'āina feeling. What fits here are things with charm, not something pristine."

Rather than adhere to a strict interpretation of old Hawai'i, Smith envisioned it as the age when islanders imported hardy pieces that had a nautical, almost industrial feel to them. "Things that had a throwaway charm to them," he says. "A bungalow style combined with native woods. That language mixed together is a very romantic style of Hawai'i."

For the guest bedroom built along a small side garden, Peacock designed outward swinging French doors and sliding 'ōhi'a shutters for privacy. Smith paired pink-hued bedding with a Chinese chest and rattan chairs. Stained concrete floors were traditionally done in red, brown, green, and less often, black. The concrete takes color unpredictably, and Peacock experimented with the Kemiko acid stain repeatedly to get the desired result.

Lanikai's Moku Iki island lies just offshore of the living room. The home's original ceiling truss was preserved but structurally improved for hurricane resistance. New 'ōhi'a doors were constructed by the Big Island's Peter Ziroli to complement the original 'ōhi'a floors, which were refinished.

As part of the new wing, the master bathroom was given an old feel with vintage details. The mermaid shower door was fabricated to match an older design and meet new safety codes, while open portholes were added to give the room character and air circulation.

Smith cites the glass mermaid panel he used as inspiration for the master bedroom shower door as an example of something that had the right feel of 1920s Hawai'i, even if it didn't have the exact pedigree. "The weird thing is that while you'd envision it found in Maui, I found it at an antique store in New York. In my mind it would have been imported to Hawaii in the Golden Age."

The children's bathroom counter is terrazzo fabricated with beach glass and mother of pearl. The stained concrete floors are made visually interesting by rotating the squares at a forty-five degree angle. The process of scoring the concrete is labor intensive, as small sections are poured and then lined by hand in the wet concrete.

town

Jonathan Staub bought this 1926 home two years ago and "simply refreshed it." He was drawn to the property on lower Tantalus, a now-extinct volcano on the edge of Honolulu's urban center, for its cool weather. "I have an aversion to air-conditioning."

THE HAWAIIAN ECLECTIC

Interior designer Jonathan Staub knows exactly what he likes in a home. "I'm all about age. I love patina," he says, noting that his greatest dislike in design is anything done for pretense.

"Whatever is put in a home should be a soulful exchange. A lot of poor design is driven by fashion. People sometimes feel they don't know what else to do, but I always remind people that they get dressed every morning and somehow make sense of it. Design is the same."

With a career that straddles Hawai'i and California, Staub's projects range from The Strand in Huntington Beach and Park La Brea in Los Angeles to the interior renovations of such classic Hawai'i hotels as the Big Island's Kona Village and Kaua'i's Coco Palms. For his personal Hawai'i residence, Staub wanted a home that had never fallen victim to the whims of fashion or a bad remodel, and in 2004 he found just that in a 1926 Tantalus hillside home that had been in the same family's possession for sixty-eight years.

"The house is so classical that I didn't want to ruin the proportions," says Staub, who chose the property in part because it's a pristine example of his favorite period in American architecture and design.

"The 1920s and '30s are when America was doing its best work. We weren't copying or replicating; we were creating. The architecture was humble in nature. It uses simple materials that don't clash with a complex environment like Hawaii's."

Staub did make changes to the residence with his distinctive use of color. When he bought the home, every wall was white. It now uses twenty-eight different colors. Only the wall's moldings were rendered in a glossy white "so that they'd really pop. They were the frosting."

When it came to furnishings, Staub already owned a vintage collection matching the architectural period.

"A lot of these pieces I've had for years and years and I may move them around but there's a tactile memory to them and there's an intimacy you'll lose when you don't hold on to things."

His library is filled with the accumulation of his collecting and that of generations of his family. "We always do libraries in our homes. It's the one place where you can be entirely eccentric, and it makes sense. It's so comforting, because it's rich and familiar. People are doing these sterile offices these days when they should be building themselves a library."

But while Staub adores tradition, he embraces it with a twist. The antique foyer set his grandmother left him sits against a shade of pistachio green which that furniture has surely never seen before. His stairwell walls are painted three different colors applied in random order between

Shell lei drape over photographs of Staub's two grandmothers. Staub is of Hawaiian descent through his maternal grandmother, pictured at her wedding.

In the library, Staub pairs a nineteenth century Tahitian *tifaifai*, or bedcover, in pink and yellow with a highboy passed down to him from his Litchfield, Connecticut, family. "You can combine New England antiques very easily in Hawai'i. Because of the missionaries, there's a context and a history for it."

Jonathan Staub's maternal grandmother, who inspired him to go into design, left him her eighteenth-century French foyer set, which now sits in his entry. The star light is Art Deco from the 1920s. In the living room are two mid-century swivel chairs designed by Edward J. Wormley. "They're probably some of the first-ever swivel chairs, which is amazing because they're so delicate," says Staub. The chairs are upholstered in fabric from Bergamo, Staub's favorite mill.

The stairwell walls were painted two tones of green and one yellow in random order. "I wrote the numbers one, two, and three on pieces of tape and didn't look as I applied them to the squares. That's how I got my sequence. The minute you have to work at random order, you ruin it."

their vintage moldings in what Staub says is a tribute to his admiration of the Partridge Family. "It harkens back to the side of their bus. I was a having a flashback to my childhood."

"I try to reach a balance in my rooms. Most people will try to partner something with its like kind, but that throws it out of balance so that what you get is a room that is slightly toxic. You get bored with the space because there's no tension. The tension between the masculine and the feminine of the color palates are what make that room actually work. People are afraid of tension, but that's what design is all about."

"The dining room has become underutilized in most homes," says Jonathan Staub, who infused the room with color using imperial plaster finish on the walls. "I find plaster has the same relationship to color that silk does. It carries it like no other construction material." Staub used fixed panel curtains because "it was unexpected and hides the window jalousies which I hate but which cool the room." The French-designed fabric includes many of the same colors used in the 1920s painting by an unknown artist which hangs beside it. The chest is a two-hundred-year-old Dutch West Indies piece.

In the living room, a 1928 Kāne'ohe Bay landscape done by the beloved Hawai'i artist David Hitchcock hangs over the fireplace. The couch is part of Staub's Wormley collection. "I love it for having an Asian-inspired notch design. It's a ten-foot-long boomerang shape, so I can float it in the room." Behind the couch is a painting by Southern folk artist Jimmy Schmit. The two coffee tables are old Chinese picnic baskets that once had gold overlay. "It's been etched off over the years by the air. If they were brand new they'd be garish, but now they're simply textured." Staub found the room's Berber rug, dyed with saffron and mint, on a week long excursion into the Sahara.

Staub's guest bed is covered with a flea-market throw found in New York. "I painted the walls a severe color to balance the bed, otherwise it would have been too frothy." Staub dislikes matching side lamps, preferring to use a mismatched pair he compares to costume. "What I love about lamps is that they're like Sunday hats. They're the character. A lot of people shy away from a lamp with character, but it's a great place to do it."

In the garden, a teak chaise and white ceramic Chinese side table. "My garden rule living in the rain forest is to work with its vitality and chaos through random integration. I like focused effort with blurred lines all around."

In the sunroom, one of two rattan and mahogany lamps purchased at the estate sale of a couple who had received them as a wedding present in the 1950s. "The wife loved champagne, and the husband preferred red wine, so that's how they got their shapes. They throw amazing patterns over the rooms at night," says Staub.

View of Jonathan Staub's deck: "The garden had an unbelievable tree canopy that I'm incredibly grateful for. It would have taken me forty years to create that."

Hawai'i is home to a fluid mix of races, but few from India have made their way to the Islands. What the Indian community lacks in numbers it makes up for in presence through the Watumull family. Arriving in Honolulu in 1914, the Watumulls originally made their name in the garment industry, leading the way in the creation of Hawaiian fabric prints that are now popular weekend wear from Los Angeles to Europe.

For Rajan and Wanda Watumull, inspiration for the renovation of their oceanfront home came from spots as disparate as Mexico, Bali and, of course, India. Their home was originally built in the early 1980s in a style that virtually ignored the phenomenal views at the home's doorstep, prompting one architect to tell them the only thing worth keeping was their Sub-Zero refrigerator.

"But I was pregnant at the time and we had nowhere else to live, so we were determined to make it work," says Wanda, who notes that starting from scratch would have been a mistake regardless. "Our tastes changed along the way, and in doing so we have been able to 'mold' the house bit by bit into what it is today. Without question something we had built ten years ago would probably not be what we enjoy now."

A small table inlaid with mother of pearl sits against temple doors brought to Hawai'i from India. The ceremonial goblets are also Indian and were used in the Watumulls' London wedding.

The Watumulls' new dining area means every meal is virtually outdoors under a high-pitched Balinese-style roof. It's a frequent spot for parties, and more than one guest has decreed they're moving to the beach after dining here. "That's really the best compliment we've received," says Wanda. The floors are Peruvian travertine.

The roofline to the left was inspired by a trip to Mexico, allowing their second floor master bedroom an unobstructed view of the ocean. Diamond Head crater rises up over the left-hand side of the house. Known to the Hawaiians as Lēʻahi, the volcanic crater became a natural landmark to weary Western travelers that their transpacific voyage was finally at an end. After a group of British sailors spotted what they thought were precious stones in its rocky soil, the slumbering crater took on its new name.

With a frontline view of a popular surf break and a row of coconut trees planted roughly one hundred years ago, the Watumulls' home lies open to the elements year round, with well-constructed floors as protection against water damage and stainless steel screens for an added layer of security. Islanders in ancient times placed torches along this shoreline to warn vessels of its reef-lined coast. The once treacherous shore capable of grounding canoes and ships is now a playground for urban Honolulu.

The Watumulls' former dining room now serves as a home theatre, with a screen that disappears into the ceiling when not in use. Their furniture is a mixture of vintage and new pieces from Southeast Asia.

They kept the bones of the house but made dramatic changes, the most powerful being the tearing down of the cedar wood wall that had blocked the home's water views. The ocean side of the house now opens permanently onto the sea and sloped grass lawn that rises up to meet it.

"I clearly remember one of the first things I wanted was the ability to eat every meal possible outside. Having been raised in London, I have very distinct memories of my father scrambling for the barbeque at the merest glimmer of sunshine, so it seemed only right in Hawai'i, where we are blessed with wonderful weather year round, that we should be able to eat outside whenever."

Having decided their indoor dining room was now a white elephant, the Watumulls recently converted it to an open air screening room. It is this room through which the visitor first enters the house, though the view of the ocean beyond is so commanding from it, the room itself almost disappears.

"I honestly believe that the thing that is most appealing about the house," says Wanda, "is the fact that the first thing you see is not the house at all but the vivid contrast of green grass, white surf break, and blue ocean. The house itself is secondary."

Wanda Watumull relaxes on a
lānai pūne‘e. This space was
formerly a solid wall cutting
the structure off from the
view. The entire lānai area
was added during the renovation to integrate the exterior
beauty of the home.

Diamond Head Crater and Waikīkī viewed from the back of Pālolo Valley.

ALOHALAND

Imagine a lifestyle that lent itself to owning three hundred aloha shirts. Dale Hope was unaware he had that many until a Japanese magazine described his closet as bursting with one hundred Hawaiian shirts, and Hope's wife bet him dinner that it had to be two, maybe three times that amount.

"That one cost me a pretty expensive night of sushi," says Hope, who grew up in the Hawaiian garment industry and took over his father's clothing business at the age of twenty-six. The search for the perfect print sent him from Hawai'i to the South Pacific.

"I'd sit under a tree in Moorea or Huahine and take pictures as people arrived from another island on the freighter. Someone would walk past in a twenty-year-old shirt that was amazing, and I'd get my all my design ideas for the next year."

The same watchful appreciation of Polynesian tradition led to his choice of home, a place he first spotted when he was a sixteen-year-old surfer hiking the back ridge of Pālolo Valley. "I saw these green, lush farms tucked up above Honolulu. Being young and poor, I got the tax map for the area and pinned it to my wall and dreamed about it."

A trio of ceramic blowfish by Jonathan Adler sits atop Hope's koa kitchen counter, which was built by a friend. On the wall, a painting that Hawai'i artist Avi Kiriaty traded with Hope in exchange for a bike Hope couldn't fit.

A painting by Avi Kiriaty hangs above a koa wood surfboard and bench. The throw pillows were found on Hope's travels through the South Pacific. The bench cushion is from Raoul textiles. A collection of glass balls, treasured mementos of early morning ocean visits in many island homes, is held in the bench's base.

In the master bathroom, photographs of surfing greats by Dr. Don James. The photos were discovered by Hope in a friend's basement and used for years in the trade show booth for his aloha shirts.

An avid surfer, Dale Hope collects books that reflect his lifelong passion for the ocean.

Twenty years after first seeing the spot, Hope was at a tiny inn on Lānaʻi when the pay phone rang with word that one of the farming families was willing to sell, and Hope finally got his piece of the valley, a spot that defies the sweltering urban center lying below it.

His neighbors are the same farmers he saw that first day when he was sixteen, and for them and himself he wanted his architecture to be island-feeling. He also needed a structure that could withstand the heavy rain showers that sweep down the back of Pālolo Valley, and so chose a pole house construction similar to those used on Oʻahu's rural North Shore as a means of elevating a home above breaking high surf.

Then a bachelor, Hope was free to create an ode to his romance with the Pacific Ocean and its islands. Irreplaceable surfboards by shaper Joe Quigg hang next to paintings by Hawaiʻi artists Yvonne Cheng and Avi Kiriaty, both of whom did textile design for Hope's former company, Kāhala Sportswear.

Hope collected quilts and pillows at art festivals in Tahiti and Rarotonga, but elected to skip a few key pieces of furniture like a dining room table. "I already had a place to sit on the deck," says Hope, "and I don't like to be indoors when you could be outdoors."

Annie Hope found the light fixture hanging over the dining room table from Tucker Robbins. Made by women in Indonesia, it is in a shape and style similar to fishing baskets used in their area. The tablecloth is from the company SeaCloth. The sideboard is an Indonesian art deco piece from Baik Design in Honolulu.

The home's missing pieces came when Hope met and married Annie Gibbons. Gibbons, who with her sister created the home fragrance line Alora Ambiance, was on vacation in Hawai'i when she first came to the home with a friend to visit Hope.

"I'd spent fifteen years in Italy and a few more in London, so I was used to a bit more of a mix of influences, but this home's heart is firmly in the islands so I knew it needed to stay that way," she says. "Plus, it was a really extraordinary place."

"She did begin the 'burn the bamboo' campaign though," laughs Hope. 'You have a little too much bamboo furniture,' she'd say."

Other than a light editing, Gibbons stayed within Dale's island theme but turned it up a notch with Polynesian prints done in linen by Santa Barbara-based Raoul Textiles and added to Hope's ocean motif with ceramic fish by New York designer Jonathan Adler.

Only when Annie became pregnant with their daughter, Ollie, did she convince Dale to add an indoor dining room table. "I told him that sometimes she would have to be indoors to do her homework."

"She made it a home," says Hope appreciatively before breaking into a chuckle to point out a bamboo bedside table that survived her purge. "Maybe she spared it because the top is made out of coconut."

A koa wood chair topped with a Raoul Textiles base cushion and a Jonathan Adler throw pillow. On the wall, a print by renowned Hawai'i artist John Kelly.

Dale Hope had Tahitian banquettes replicated for the family's lānai, where he and daughter Ollie breakfast every morning. Shells arranged above the seats were found during Hope's ocean swims.

In a scene repeated at nearly every doorway in the state, slippers pile up at the Hopes' front door, where heliconia, monstera, and ti picked on the property greet visitors. Hope's pineapple sign was created by friend Steve Neil.

Ollie's bed is covered with a quilt bought at the Rarotonga Art Festival. The vintage lamp to the right is a carved-wood ulua fish, and on the wall above it is a block print from one of Hope's aloha shirt designs. The Waikiki Surfriders sign is by Steve Neil. Annie Hope's first "child" Gigi sits in the middle of it all. A street dog Annie rescued while living in Italy, Gigi relocated to Hawai'i when her mother moved to the Islands to marry Dale.

A fanciful Hawaiian scene from one of Hope's three hundred aloha shirts. This fabric, and the more traditional Polynesian prints used throughout the home, are both descendents ultimately of the tapa prints created by Polynesians before Western contact. Their graphic printed designs done on beaten bark cloth were copied and reinterpreted on cotton fabric by textile manufacturers, giving rise to the Tahitian pareu and the Hawaiian aloha shirt.

Dale, Annie, and Ollie Hope walk the lush path up to their Pālolo Valley home.

"We knew we had a rare and magnificent site," wrote Betty Liljestrand in 1958, the year *House Beautiful* devoted an entire issue to her family's mountainside home. "We wanted to be able to sit inside, listen to good music and, with the lights dimmed, take full advantage of the fairy-like city below us."

That Dr. and Mrs. Howard Liljestrand built a house in Hawai'i at all was a stroke of historical luck. They'd been en route to China in the late 1930s when political turmoil forced them to relocate to Hawai'i, where Dr. Liljestrand became an Oahu plantation physician. The family lived for nearly a decade in remote spots surrounded by miles of sugar cane before finding the Tantalus perch that would become their permanent home.

"We hiked through the hills," wrote Betty Liljestrand in her 1958 notes, "admiring the changing views from one ridge to the next. Here land was relatively undeveloped."

Thanks to the fact that much of Tantalus has been set aside as forest reserve, it remains largely undeveloped. The tremendous growth of the city below it has made the Lijestrand's setting all the more dramatic. Built a thousand feet above Honolulu on a marvelous acre of eucalyptus trees, their house still captures the imagination of design enthusiasts fifty years after its construction due to architect Vladimir Ossipoff's innovative plan.

Eucalyptus trees surround the redwood deck, copper gutters, and chimney. The balcony rail serves both as a safety measure and built-in seating without obstructing views. The sliding doors connecting exterior with interior were one of Ossipoff's trademarks.

Born in Russia, raised in Japan, and educated at UC Berkeley, Ossipoff came to Hawai'i in the early 1930s ready to combine California's modernist movement with a Japanese sense of craftsmanship and materials. During his sixty-year career in Hawai'i, he was dubbed by some to be the Frank Lloyd Wright of warm-weather shelter, designing major public spaces, over a thousand homes, and changing the way many island residents wanted to live.

"He evolved the sense of Hawaiian architecture to the point that people are still learning from him," says Nate Smith, one of a new generation of up-and-coming Honolulu architects who cite Ossipoff as a primary influence. "His homes were made of the finest native stone, copper, wood, glass, and steel. He blended them in a way that was respectful and understated."

The Betty and Howard Liljestrand residence is one of the purest examples of Ossipoff's aesthetic. Built in 1952, the home has been left virtually unchanged since. Its dark woods, deep overhangs, oversized windows, and huge sliding doors are textbook Ossipoff.

Ossipoff visited the Liljestrand property every week during the two-year design process. His slow study of the site shows in the home's grounded presence among the trees. Each room has a perfectly framed view, and every tree possible was left standing by curving in the lines of the master wing.

The structure seems nestled into the mountainside, yet open to the views of the rainforest, city, and ocean that spread around it.

Ossipoff, who was born in Vladivostok, Russia, in 1907 and died in Honolulu ninety-one years later, was known for his perfect framing of Hawaiian views, as in this case with Diamond Head Crater and Waikīkī. "He placed a window at a sill height that would block the house below it and also emphasize the view," says architect Nate Smith. "He knew how you were going to live in a home, knew where you should place the chair to enjoy the view."

The living room furniture was designed under Ossipoff's exacting eye. The guava tree branch which serves as the table base was harvested by Dr. Liljestrand from the surrounding forest.

In the open-air pavilion play-room Ossipoff designed for the four Liljestrand children on the home's first floor sits a custom-made Ping-Pong table which Ossipoff decreed should be painted to match the poured concrete floor.

An evening view of the house elevation. The runway lights of Honolulu International Airport glow between the tree branches.

Ossipoff's attention to detail extended beyond the setting to the smallest aspects of the furnishings. Unsatisfied with what he saw on the market, he designed much of Liljestrands' furniture, mocking it up in cardboard before it was built. Deciding he would create a coffee table from a piece of rain-forest wood, he sent Dr. Liljestrand into the Tantalus forest with instructions to find a piece of guava wood with three branches pointing upward and three pointing down. "When my dad managed to find it, Val [Ossipoff's nickname] had the tabletop mocked up on butcher paper with the order that it not be done in glass," says the Lijestrands' son Bob. "He specified it be done in Plexiglas because he thought the greenish tint of glass would be jarring in the room."

Ossipoff's perfectionism was shared by Betty Liljestrand, who served as the home's general contractor during its two years of construction. Working with the two Japanese master craftsmen Ossipoff chose for the job, Liljestrand learned to say "stop" in Japanese whenever she saw work not to her liking. "She would then call Ossipoff, who was fluent in Japanese, and explain the problem," says Bob Liljestrand.

"He'd get on the phone to the carpenters. Mom soon learned to recognize the grumbled Japanese response, 'Here we go, tear it out.'"

The four-year process paid off, with *House Beautiful* effusing in its forty-seven page coverage of the residence that, "when you sense every day that you are moving about within a piece of hollowed sculpture, you are experiencing one of the greatest values a house can give."

In her personal notes, Betty Liljestrand described the sensation of being at home in a more modest voice, one befitting a creation of the eminently understated Vladimir Ossipoff. "The view and the weather are as much a part of this house as the walls and roof," she wrote. "The house keeps us in touch with the sea, sky, and things that grow."

The redwood dining room walls are done in the classic Ossipoff treatment of rubbed-off paint finish. The family's china was chosen by Dr. and Mrs. Liljestrand to enhance the room's Japanese screen. The gold alloy plates were done by Dirilyte Co. Sterling flatware, the goblets were by West Virginia Glass Co. The living room walls are made of—now environmentally unthinkable—harvested sandstone from Yokohama Bay on the West side of O'ahu. "In those days," says Bob Liljestrand, "they simply went out with a bulldozer and dragged it up."

A Japanese screen hangs in the dining room. Ossipoff set small reading lights, like those used on airlines, into the room's ceiling to cover the table with a pool of light, believing that larger fixtures would destroy the room's lines. The architect also designed the ten-foot-long oak dining room table. Hans Wegner chairs were refinished to match it.

The bedroom was built at an angle so that no trees would need to be cut. Ossipoff was known for the built-in cabinetry of his homes. These built-ins are fashioned out of a monkeypod tree Dr. Liljestrand found plantation workers dousing with gasoline because it shed too much. After offering to have it removed, he had a windfall of material for the stairs, countertops, and much of the furniture throughout the home.

In 1958, *House Beautiful* wrote that though the home was built in the Territory of Hawai'i, it has meaning to anyone living on the mainland of the USA. "Every family building a new house cherishes a dream of bringing together ordinary things like stone, wood, glass, concrete, and pipe in such a way that these will add up to a whole that is greater than the obvious sum of the parts."

Hāpu'u ferns provide a shady canopy at the home's entrance. Ossipoff's integration of Hawaii's natural setting continues to inspire island architects.

A study in greens: a ceramic
Chinese ventilation tile punc-
tuates the lichen-tinted fence
adjacent to the driveway.

country

The Twigg-Smiths' 1895
shingle and lava rock home.
Christian's family has been in
Kona for six generations.
His great-great-great grand
parents Reverend Asa and Lucy
Thurston, pioneer missionaries to Hawai'i in 1820, built
one of the islands' original
lava-rock structures using
coral which, when heated with
fire, became limestone mortar.
The ruins of the homesite,
known as Laniākea, lie just
a few miles away from this
home. The Reverend Asa
Thurston is credited with
building Moku'aikaua Church
in the village of Kailua-Kona
in 1839.

At first glance, the cool, upland Kona home of Lisa and
Christian Twigg-Smith is simply inviting. It's a tribute to the
understated grace of this couple that only after an hour
or more in their home does the tremendous legacy of their
families begin to register with the visitor. A painting by
renowned Hawai'i artist Charles Bartlett hangs quietly outside, as if hung for the ti and ginger plants to enjoy. Wooden
furniture passed down from Lisa's great-grandparents, Oahu
Sugar plantation manager August Ahrens and Louisa Hapai
Ahrens, stands in testament to the skill of a Japanese sugar
plantation carpenter nearly a century ago. A lauhala pune'e,
or day bed, from her part-Hawaiian grandmother sits on
the lānai. Scenes of Hawai'i landscapes from a by-gone era
painted by Christian's grandfather William Twigg-Smith,
hang in the dining room. There's no effort to recapture old
Hawai'i here, because it's never been lost.

Tradition is paramount to the Twigg-Smiths. "So much so that
sometimes it takes years to move *tutu's* (grandma's) couch
because 'it's always been there,'" laughs Lisa.

Christian's Honolulu grandparents bought the home sight
unseen during World War II and arrived to a house badly in
need of work. Originally built in 1895 by Manual Goularte
Silva, who raised many of his fourteen children there, it had
been left uninhabited for many years. Most of the structure's
renovations were done by "Grandpa Twigg" and sons David
and Thurston after 1945. "They couldn't get materials readily

123

Through the simple screened door entry, a view of ti and ginger. The home is surrounded by gardenia bushes, and the property was once crossed by an *alanui* (path). One of many in the area, it was used as a foot trail to link mountain and ocean communities in Kona's steep terrain.

in Kona because of war shortages. Now if we do repairs we see that behind the 1940s canec paneling, part of the wall support is of patched, recycled lumber. That was the material they had to work with," says Lisa. During those post-war years, the family was unable to get hardwood flooring, and Lisa and Christian have kept the masonite floors that Christian's family finished to look like stained concrete, pairing it with lauhala mats.

The home's pink color is further testament to the family's comfort with the past. "Grandpa Twigg gets credit for the house being pink," says Lisa. "He found a very old piece of railing board painted that color under the house. Pink was a popular color in Kona in the 1940s as well as around the turn of the century when this was originally built, so he decided to keep that color."

His son, David Twigg-Smith, carried on his father's pink tradition to his Hilo property, where he and wife Benedict raised a family of seven. The Hilo property is a more free-spirited version of the Twigg-Smith's aesthetic. Family art hangs on wallpapered walls that no one's changed since they were kids. As Christian says, "It makes the place feel as good as a well-worn shoe."

The Twigg-Smith's Tahitian relatives spend quiet time there each summer, reconnecting with the Hawai'i clan, stringing lei and surfing. Friends and overflow family stay in the guest house David Twigg-Smith painted pink in honor of his mother's and father's homestead on the Kona side of the island.

Bottles found at old Kona sites line the downstairs shelves. Bottle digging was a poular pastime in Hawai'i in the 1960s.

In the Kona dining room hang a collection of Grandpa Twigg's landscapes. William Twigg-Smith supported his family as an illustrator for the Hawai'i Sugar Planters Association. A thin, lanky man who immigrated to Hawai'i from New Zealand, his nickname was Twigg, which he added to his surname of Smith when he became a US citizen. A Deborah Butterfield sculpture sits on the floor below.

The family Kona kitchen floors are new vinyl in the old Hawai'i style. The rest of the floors on this level are the original masonite fashioned to look like concrete. Wartime restrictions meant a lack of other building materials, and Lisa and Christian have seen no reason to change it, though they have remodeled the kitchen for more modern uses.

In the living room, Lisa's "soul piece," her grandmother's lauhala pune'e. The pune'e is descended from the practice of stacking lauhala mats atop one another for a soft spot to relax on.

The Hilo pink guesthouse,
colored to honor the Kona
tradition of the family.

A visiting Tahitian relative of the Twigg-Smith family at rest in the Hilo living room.

The view from the family's Hilo living room out to the ancient shoreline of hala trees, rock, and sea.

The Hilo kitchen is one many a kamaʻāina would feel at home in.

The children's playhouse and beds were designed by Edward Mitchell of London, Benedict Twigg-Smith's architect father. The playhouse features a bed for naps, books for story time, and miniature rooms complete with picture windows.

Children's bunk beds are built cleverly on an angle because of a stairwell below.

The rest of the family stays in the main house, which also reflects David's ingenuity. An engineer for what was then Ola'a Sugar, David rescued three plantation houses from demolition in the 1960s when one of the plantation camps was closing, adding them to what had been a very tiny house at the end of the road in Keaukaha. "With a fast-growing family, they certainly needed the space, and they accomplished it in such a resourceful way for the time," adds Lisa.

The Hilo home is still in tune with the needs of the littlest Twigg-Smiths and their friends. Their favorite feature is a "built to half-scale," two-story children's playhouse designed and constructed at the time of the add-on of three plantation houses by Benedict's father Edward Mitchell of London. Embedded in the heart of the home, the playhouse is a touch of their other grandparent from faraway England.

"The little cousins all adore it. They play, nap, and read in there all day. It's the highlight of a visit for them. This house is about the family."

A summer volleyball game
on the lawn.

Carved lava rocks found along
the rugged coastlines of the
Big Island, used for salt making or kōnane, a game similar
to checkers.

Surrounding the children at play is ocean and old growth
hala trees. It's a landscape that can feel gentle or powerful,
but always ancient. A Hawaiian grave is honored and left
undisturbed in the lava-rock walls between the home and
the ocean.

"Without doubt, this place has mana (spiritual power) about
it. The family has had Hawaiian elders on the property.
They tell us that this site has a history of good things, and
good people. There's not a better feeling than that."

The main house, the original section of which was picked up and moved six feet back by the 1946 Hilo tsunami.

The Baldwin property's main house is trellised with roses that grow wild in the pasture, thriving in upcountry Maui's cooler weather. "People stop to tell us that they came here once to pick blackberries, as a visitor to a party, picnic, or hike," says Sally Baldwin. "We are blessed to be here."

Built high on the slope of Haleakalā, Edward and Sally Baldwin's home is not easily reached. Visitors must travel along miles of Olinda's wooded pastures before reaching a dirt road that rambles through the Baldwins' twenty-eight acres of eucalyptus forest, ending at their rose-covered cottage named Idlewild. Neither the cottage nor this part of Maui has changed significantly in the last century, and the trip feels as if it should be made by horse and wagon.

"The best thing about living here is the timelessness of it," says Edward Baldwin, who grew up down the road in Makawao. "I remember we used to come up to pick blackberries here. We'd make the trip up the winding road then through the gate. It felt like a great adventure."

Edward Baldwin is the fourth generation of his family to live at Idlewild. His missionary great-great-great grandfather, Dr. Dwight Baldwin, arrived in Maui from New England in 1834, founding what became one of Maui's most prominent families. But it was Edward's great-great uncle, James Alexander, who built Idlewild in the 1870s. Stylistically, it is virtually untouched, with the same single-wall construction it was given over 130 years ago.

The Baldwins' dining room is warmed by the heat of an Aga oven. Beyond the windows are roses and mountain ferns, as well as views of the West Maui Mountains and Lana'i.

The koa bed is a family heirloom. "When my family came here they had New England-style furniture made out of local materials, like this koa," says Edward. The bed was originally a rope bed with a straw mattress.

"The roof's been made of tin as long as anyone can remember," says Edward, who replaced the foundation and plumbing. "We built trellising to lift the roses off the windows, but otherwise we've tried to leave it the way people have always enjoyed it."

Believed to be one of the oldest continually inhabited homes in Hawai'i, Idlewild's guest book testifies to its pedigree, reading like a directory of some of Hawai'i's oldest families: the von Tempskys were Idlewild's first recorded visitors, and the Damons and Cookes signed in along with Governor Samuel Dole, who on his departure wrote of Idlewild: "Sheltering groves and evening star/Purple dawns for watching eyes/Warring clouds in frowning skies."

An entry from February 17, 1907 records a hail storm, and on October 8, 1907, the Atherton family writes appreciatively: "This day we ascended from the lower country the family to spend at least three weeks in the cool of the mountains." They traveled lightly, bringing a maid, cook, seven horses, one cow, one calf, and a single cat.

Today, life at Idlewild follows many of the same joys nineteenth-century visitors described: days of berry picking, admiring Haleakalā's beauty, and nights of cool weather.

"Idlewild is consistently twenty degrees cooler than Kahului, and we've had frost before when the temperature drops into the 30s," says Sally Baldwin, who purchased an Aga stove

The Baldwins' lānai con-
structed with the traditional
Hawaiian crosshatch pattern.
The single-wall construction
is original to the home. The
board and batten was added
twenty years ago, as were
the homemade windows.
Sally and Edward have used
much of the property's twenty-
eight acres to rebuild the
fruit orchard and flower
beds Baldwin's family wrote
of in their journal over a
century ago.

Edward Baldwin's cousin added these handmade windows to the home. Each is a slightly different size. Despite the often chilly weather, the couple uses a shower just outside year round.

for the house from England after she learned it could be kept on round the clock for heat. "On a cold night we just sit around it." Edward and Sally enjoy their own history with the house, having shared it as their first home after marriage, returning only recently. "When we were first married, Edward's Tutu (grandmother) owned it, and we were caretakers. We started our family here," says Sally. After corporate work took their family to the mainland for twenty years, they came full circle, returning to Maui to settle down at Idlewild for good.

"It is remote living," says Sally. "We're behind a gate and up a dirt road. But it's all worth it. We are blessed to live here and we take the time to appreciate it every day."

"All these years later it's still a great place to explore," says Edward. "I just found wild walnut trees in a nearby gulch. It's a part of Maui with deep roots for my family, and it's as close to untouched as you can find these days."

The caretaker's cottage, to the left, and barn lie at the edge of the property's eucalyptus forest. A hāpu'u fern stands in the foreground. "At one point this was a halfway point for horseback rides up and into Haleakalā Crater. There used to be a stable next to the cottage, and we still find the occasional horseshoe in the flower beds by the cottage."

This sink, which was originally in the main house, has been moved into the cottage. Kukui nut and shell lei as well as a hibiscus painting hang on the wall.

Just one generation ago a caretaker, his wife, and three children made their home in this single-room structure. The three sons still return to the property to retell stories of their remote childhood there.

The small chandelier and leopard-print chairs provide a note of glamour in the otherwise homespun cottage setting.

Evening clouds, propelled by the prevailing trade winds, fly over Idlewild. "Nobody seems to know the origin of the name," says Edward when asked about the significance of "Idlewild." Haleakalā is just upslope of the 1870s home, with only a eucalyptus forest separating the house from the dormant volcano.

"This is probably the last quiet place to live in Hawai'i where there is a rainforest," says artist Laka Morton, whose cabin is nestled in the native red-blossomed 'ōhi'a trees and deep green hāpu'u ferns that surround Volcanoes National Park on the Big Island. Picturesque Volcano Village is the only town for miles, and both the psychology and geography of the area are dominated not by the workaday aspects of business and tourism, but rather the dramatic activity of Kīlauea Volcano.

Morton moved here in 1992 after Hurricane Iniki hit his native Kaua'i. He chose Volcano for its remoteness. Morton didn't want to live among high rises, and the highest thing here is the dense vegetation that shadows and cools his home even in midday. He uses a wood stove burner to heat the room when company is over or on very cold nights.

Morton built the home with the help of a neighbor with wood they found at the local dump. "We cleared paths through the fern grotto to build. I just wanted to build something simple. I don't need all the space. My sense of luxury is my home, my things."

The stenciled beam in the ceiling was inspired by a Chinese design. The wall design was inspired by the split bamboo exteriors of old Tahitian homes.

The shell lei are made of Styrofoam balls and bamboo reeds. In his first year of making them, Morton made over a hundred and gave them away. "I thought it was so sad that the shells were usually just used in tacky things to sell to tourists. I wanted to see them be made into something beautiful."

"I need quiet and solitude if I'm going to paint and create," says Morton. "I'd rather create than socialize." The bright oils of his portraits cut the darkness, as do the sheen of his shell mosaics. The walls of his bathroom exhibit decades' worth of collecting on Kauai's once shell-laden beaches.

"Every day I would wake up at dawn, grab my basket. It was a great way to start the day, to be in nature looking for free treasure. All the shells on the bathroom walls are from Hāʻena."

The split bamboo exteriors of old Tahitian houses inspired the pattern of Morton's living room. "It took me three months to paint, which people always say is a lot, but it's easier than splitting the bamboo and weaving it," Morton chuckles.

"The walls took three weeks to glue but years to find," says Morton, who glued the shells to panels, which he then adhered to the walls.

A fragrant angel's trumpet tree provides a graceful backdrop for the pond Morton dug in the rainforest behind his house.

An almost otherworldly sense of Hawai'i is present in Laka's bedroom. Outside, a field of kāhili ginger blooms a fluorescent gold in the mist of the volcanic forest. This is the legendary ground of Hawaii's fire goddess Pele, and Morton's portrait of her looks out toward the volcano she is believed to control.

"I was hesitant to paint Pele. For me it was like painting God," says Morton. "How do you know what she looks like? All you can do is define it as you would see her image pass. It changes with every glance, it's all in your interpretation and it's not always right and won't always please everyone, not even yourself."

In the hush of Volcano, Morton has the peace to muse on the presentation of Pele, when so much of Hawai'i has become too busy to think of ancient legends at all. "If you know what you don't like, don't live near it," says Morton. "The whole world has a pulse and if you can find a space where you hear it, and it's quiet, you're so fortunate. This is as close to paradise as I can take."

A portrait of the Hawaiian goddess Pele sits in Morton's bedroom, where painted pressboard coated with tinted resin makes for a textured treatment of red that contrasts with the green forest outside. "I always loved red," says Morton. "Aries, I guess."

A field of kāhili ginger bloom in the forest outside Laka's bedroom. When the kāhili is in season, all of Volcano is filled with its heady fragrance.

ARTISTS IN RESIDENCE

Artist Doug Britt has worked as an artist in Kaua'i for twenty-five years, selling his oil paintings in the charming north shore town of Hanalei. But when Britt first arrived in Hawai'i in 1968, it was as a runaway teenager. Then a surf-obsessed high school student, he'd left his parents' home undetected and flown to Honolulu alone. "Of course, four days later he called his parents and they sent him a ticket home," Britt's wife Sharon explains.

His draw to the islands continued. While attending the San Francisco Art Institute in the 1970s, Doug scouted property on Maui. Deciding he couldn't afford it, he flew to Kaua'i and bought an oceanside parcel the day after he arrived. Having married Sharon, who had herself followed a pack of surfer friends to Kaua'i in the mid-seventies, Doug decided to trade in their beach property in 1988 to build in the mountains of Kalihiwai Ridge.

"Doug wanted more room to build a studio and working space," says Sharon. "There was no road up here at the time. We had to come through the guava fields. We did not even have the full grasp of our view. Doug purchased a tractor and worked for two years. Every time we saw a little bit more of the view we were shocked. We were on the edge of a valley with no civilization in sight, only mountains and water-falls and beautiful sky."

A Doug Britt oil inspired by the moon hangs against the dining room wall. Doug made the chairs out of apple plywood. The floor is poured concrete, and the exposed beam roof is raw Douglas fir.

From the bedroom lānai, a spectacular view of Kalihiwai Valley and the Hanalei mountain range. The property was initially so overgrown, the Britts were unaware of the vista their home would provide.

151

On the front porch, two Adirondack chairs made by a friend sit beneath a painting of the Hawaii state seal. The large glass balls were found on north shore Kaua'i beaches.

The couple's home was inspired by their lifelong interest in Hawaiian plantation homes.

They asked Doug's architect father to design a home for them influenced by "old Hawai'i." "We'd looked at plantation homes for years on all the islands," says Sharon. "We were both kind of obsessed by them. We feel very lucky to have lived in the last years of Hawaii's plantation days and are carrying on that legacy of living simply in a single-wall cane house."

But the romance of simple living stood the ultimate test just months after they moved in when Hurricane Iniki hit Kaua'i on September 11, 1992. The Britts were traveling on Maui when it arrived, and it was Doug's brother who got up at dawn to board up their brand new house.

"We pleaded with him from Maui to go to the house next door, because it was concrete. He introduced himself to the neighbors and they took him in. [The neighbors'] house was severely damaged and they thought our house would be completely gone. To their great surprise, our little wooden plantation house was just fine. There are all kinds of theories on why houses made it or not. We have plenty of them."

In the Britts' afternoon dream corner, a day bed built by Doug is complemented by his oils and the gift of a pillow made by their artist neighbor Pam Lightfoot.

An exhuberant detail of one of Doug Britt's paintings.

In the Britts' living room, Doug's oil of an outrigger canoe hangs over a desk he fashioned from an 1898 piano found on Kaua'i. The desk is filled with a collection of the couple's Hawaiiana. The ships on top of the piano case were woven by Sharon.

Having survived the hurricane, the Britts' home became what they'd imagined it to be: a vibrant art space. In 1994, their creative work in the home was the subject of their two-person show at the Honolulu Contemporary Museum featuring Sharon's photographs of old Hawai'i and Doug's furniture.

The show kicked off a furniture spree for Doug. Their residence is now filled with chairs and desks that began their lives as old pianos or electric poles. With the exception of some vintage pieces, everything is made by Doug's hands.

"We have edited almost everything out of our lives except art, books, and things with great meaning. In the late afternoon when the light floods our house, we may just kick back, listen to some music, and enjoy Doug's paintings. Living in Hawai'i is like living nowhere else. It is not for everyone. We have watched hundreds of people come and go. The remoteness works for us. It is what Doug paints about. It is what I put in my weaving and photos. It is our sanctuary."

Doug Britt's studio stands at the edge of this natural pond. He paints here at dawn.

The meandering road through the Britts' property is planted with a mixture of green- and red-hued plants. "We love the contrast and balance of those colors in nature."

On the top of the property's
hill, the Britts' view of sunrise,
sunset, and passing weather.

Doug Britt's studio sits in a separate structure on the property. His paintings are inspired by living in the middle of the Pacific Ocean. "Sometimes if we have not traveled in a while, we have to force ourselves to go or else we may never leave."

forces of nature

THE FLOATING HOUSE

During his long career as a hotel developer, Georg Rafael had worked with such renowned architects as Ed Killingsworth and I. M. Pei. But when it came time to design his personal residence in Hawaiʻi, he says the choice of architect Edward Tuttle seemed obvious.

"We liked his approach to the tropics and the Pacific," says Rafael. "When we approached him about this we told him we wanted a Hawaiian-influenced home. It had to be transparent: an open house with a pitched roof and porches. But basically, we gave him a free hand."

Tuttle, who is well known as the designer of many of the Aman resorts, had already designed a villa for Georg and his wife Rosie at the Amanpuri in Phuket. But the Hawaiʻi project required an entirely different approach.

"I try to design for the climate and cultural attitudes, mainly in respect to function and aesthetics," says Tuttle. "The Amanpuri villas are basically a series of pavilions, pools, and water gardens located on suspended terraces. The Rafael's Hawaiʻi residence is basically one structure opening and integrating with the exterior wherever possible. The limited size of the property and the required functions, along with setback regulations, really created the architectural envelope as one structure outside of the guest house."

A modernist pavilion defined by two massive coral plinths bisects a traditional Hawaiian roofline. These massive coral walls provide structural support as well as housing the home's mechanical systems. Tuttle designed the swimming pool to act as a reflecting pool from the living room.

Bronze skylights cast a precise pattern of shadows on the French limestone floors. Although a historic building material for Hawai'i, the home's white coral, seen here on the wall, was harvested in the Philippines due to current ocean conservation laws.

From the pool, the living room connects through a breezeway to the front entry. "It's indoor to outdoor and flows freely but is also protected," says Tuttle. "That is Hawaiian-style living."

An open walkway lined with teak pillars wraps around the house to provide protection to the rooms once doors slide open. "One of the most exciting aspects of the house is that its corners are transparent," says Tuttle. "The system presented the challenge of creating a very open house yet one that can be easily sealed for security."

The Rafaels' infinity edge pool with Koko Head in the background. The pool tiles were handmade in Thailand and installed by craftsmen from Portugal.

Although this was the first project Tuttle had ever undertaken in Hawai'i, he had visited the Islands throughout his life and immediately chose white coral as a classic Hawaiian building material for the home.

"It's a strikingly exotic material which I have seen used in Hawai'i for many years. It feels very appropriate for the culture," says Tuttle. "It's probably not a material I would use in Thailand." Beyond the difference in materials, Tuttle notes that the Rafael's Phuket home was based on the concept of hotel living, while their Hawai'i house has been designed with what he terms a more suburban attitude, though it too is located on the beach in a tropical climate.

That tropical climate inspired Tuttle to design two massive interior walls that hide the building's infrastructure and provide all of its structural support, allowing every exterior wall of the building to open up entirely to the ocean and gardens. Rafael calls this a "floating transparency."

"It's the most striking feature. It's all movable. Every corner opens up. That transparency, the light, it's fantastic," says Rafael. "It's very unique. Very Ed Tuttle."

164

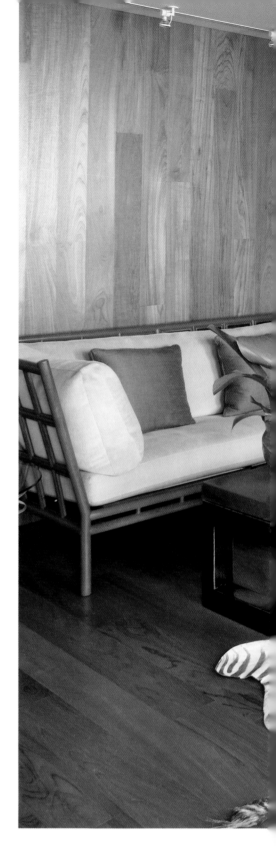

Ming anthuriums sit atop the guest room bathtub, which appears to "float." Tuttle had its base fabricated out of mirrors.

Tuttle brought the ceiling down low in this guest room suite, due to height limitations. As a way of expanding the space, the guest suite uses the combination of wood and mirrors familiar to guests at the Tuttle-designed Amanpuri resort in Phuket.

The stunning teak stairwell was almost an afterthought. The Rafaels wanted to use the upper space of the home as a guest suite, and Rafael suggested an independent stairwell to make the guest entrance separate.

A portrait by renowned
Hawai'i artist John Young is
framed by bronze powder-
coated doors leading into
the master suite.

A grid of cement pavers and
grass leads to the home's main
entrance and then around to
a separate guest cottage.

This LED-illuminated ledge
lights up at night, encircling
the structure with a glowing
band of glass. Though
Tuttle has used similar light
boxes in other projects, this
is a custom design.

The ceiling was done in duck fir because the owner wanted it whitewashed. His taste for animal prints in his fashion line carries over to the home's sparse furnishings.

HOUSE OF STONE

If James Bond lived in Hawai'i, it would be here. Crafted primarily out of rock from Maui's fields and rivers, this Spreckelsville home is modern, masculine, and anything but a whimsical Hawaiian beach house.

"I know how fast everything goes in these conditions," says the owner. "I knew I wanted rock, glass, and a wood roof. No plaster, no sheetrock. I wanted something heavy and lasting."

A sportswear designer and former professional skier from Switzerland, the owner arrived in Hawai'i twenty-five years ago to windsurf. After five years of renting and spending his days surfing the beach outside his present home, he decided to buy the property from singer Willie Nelson when it was just "a little place on the rocks amidst a field of kiawe."

The owner began to sketch plans for a structure based on octagons, a form he'd liked the use of in Japanese architecture. The sketches were a rough draft of the three octagon structure the house became when Maui architect Tim Farrington took the concept and ran with it.

"To start with a specific piece of geometry and have to build around it is unusual," Farrington says. "Design is usually determined by use and setting."

The octagon-based design of the home is inspired by the owner's travels in Japan. A lānai encircles the house, allowing the family to watch the ocean. Knowing that he was building in a tsunami zone, the owner chose a heavy foundation, rock walls, and "a lot of redwood that can survive the ocean winds."

Evidence of the owner's passion for windsurfing is glimpsed on the lawn. A local artist constructed the chimney and bathrooms of river rock.

Farrington created one octagon that functioned as the living room, with two others on either side that are used as bedrooms. The only exception is the kitchen, which is wedged between two of the octagons as a linear connector.

The octagon concept proved a perfect fit for the weather conditions. "Winds come tearing down that coastline," says Farrington. "That's why the windsurfers are there. We had to allow the winds to come through the home for ventilation, but it also had to be a windbreak. That's what the octagon allowed us to do. It brings the wind around the structure."

Because the building lies within a tsunami zone, it had to be fifteen feet off the ground and disguise a very elaborate structure of concrete mat going down six feet below sea level

and rising twelve feet above finished grade. "It's a tremendous amount of concrete and steel," adds Farrington. "Before we started the stone work, it looked like a postmodern building."

But while the design is unusual for the islands, Farrington cites the shake roof and open beam as Hawaiian influences, noting that with its sliding doors and louvered ventilation system, the house is something his client could not have built outside of the tropics. "He couldn't put that home in Switzerland; he'd freeze. It's very adaptable to its environment."

Built seventeen years ago for 2.2 million dollars, the owner estimates the project would likely cost triple that figure to build today. "That mahogany staircase would be very difficult to replicate now," says Farrington, referring to the spiral staircase running from the entry to living room and resembling a string of DNA. "The workmanship is incredible."

Both the staircase and river rock walls were the owner's ideas. While successful, the choices made the architecture immensely challenging.

The home's entry was originally entirely exposed to the outside before the owner chose to glass it in for neatness.

The house, including these mahogany stairs inspired by a photograph the owner saw in a book, was constructed entirely by Maui craftsmen, many of whom were working at a pineapple cannery at the time.

Shoji doors and river rock combine for a Japanese-inspired master bathroom.

After accumulating nearly four acres of land piece by piece, the owner set about designing a landscape "somewhere between Japanese and tropical." This corner of the pool was designed to replicate the shallowness of a beach, making it safer for children.

"The problem with being an architect is that you have to be practical," says Farrington. "River rock is a very difficult medium to do well. Coral stone is a much easier material to work with. River rock is very heavy. It's very round. There's a tendency to put too much grout on it. You have to sit the rocks really well so you don't have to use a lot of grout. And to go up into the cane fields and haul this stuff out is by no means an easy task."

"But I'd have to say that in thirty years I've only had two or three projects that went as well as this one did. Sometimes you need to have a client who lets you think out of the box. It inspires and challenges you to take things to the next level."

THE RIDGE HOUSE

The Winer home sits beneath a World War II pillbox bunker perched atop Ka Iwi Ridge. Lanikai's beach was barricaded with barbed wire and manned with lookouts throughout the war as a precaution following the attack on Pearl Harbor.

Bromeliads as catnip. Vincent had the kitchen counters fabricated in a blue-toned German green stone to incorporate the garden ocean tones surrounding the property.

Tucked into Lanikai's Ka Iwi Ridge, the home of Andy Winer and Michele Varin is literally tied to its surroundings.

"Some of the ridge is left uncovered and protrudes into the house," says architect Peter Vincent, who remodeled the home in 2001. The house was originally built in 1970 by Alvin Badenhop, a student of Frank Lloyd Wright.

Badenhop finished a portion of the hillside with cement, using it as an entry wall into the home. "It's a classic Frank Lloyd Wright trademark," adds Vincent. "Usually Wright used a fireplace or chimney. Here it's a wall through which the earth is extending into the home. The house is anchored to the hill with this concrete and rock wall, yet it cantilevers out with more contemporary, light elements, like full height glass walls and a lānai extending out toward the ocean."

"It's a design that's perfect for a hillside lot that has interesting geographical features," says owner Andy Winer, who notes another Wright characteristic of the house in its placement halfway down the slope, or on the "brow" of the hillside. The structure's position in the middle of the sloped lot is the Winers' favorite aspect of the architecture, allowing them to experience different levels of the property. The top level opens onto the boulders and surrounding ocean, while the lower level gives them the privacy of trees with an ocean view.

The original rock and cement wall at the entry is joined by a recently added red accent wall at the end of the hall. Vincent used black granite with a flamed finish on the entry stairs to contrast with the rock wall.

Vincent changed the ceiling from painted beams with burlap to split pine with a light stain finish.

When Vincent first saw the home, it was "wonderful, but very dark," he says. "It felt cluttered. The wind rattled through it, and it leaked. It had been built on a shoestring budget and in the 1960s with a more bohemian mind-set in contrast to Lanikai's present property costs."

Built into the earth, the structure allowed bugs and termites to enter at will. The house felt cluttered, and while the views were impressive, they were nearly impossible to enjoy. If a visitor's eyes adjusted to the dark interior, they were blinded by the view. Vincent's design challenge was to lighten up the interior so that it felt like part of the outside without destroying the character of the house.

Faced with a patchwork of different building materials in the home, the Winers tore out white floor tiles and rattling window panes, opting for picture windows and a neutral palette to match the simplicity of the structure's lines. Vincent chose light wood flooring and matching cabinetry to minimize those features and accent the concrete wall and landscape. He installed more sophisticated doors and windows for greater openness to views. The original ceiling of dark-stained burlap was changed to wood-slatted material to add texture and rhythm.

"The balancing of exterior and interior brightness allows the eye to move out of the home toward the rocks, wind, and sea which make this home feel otherworldly," says Vincent.

"It is a very spiritual place," adds Michele Varin. "People tell us they can feel that when they come here." From their deck, the Winers have watched whales and meteor showers, as well as the nesting of shearwaters.

"There's an interesting spirit at the house," agrees Vincent. "That's something that we tried to retain and enhance. This place definitely had something to it, and we just brought it up to date and let a cleaner design allow it to come through."

From the deck, the tiny island of Moku Iki lies offshore. Landscaper Leland Miyano chose a monochromatic palate of blue-toned plants to echo the ocean. "I wanted a difference in textures: the star shape of agave, or century plant, and the flow of ʻākia, which breaks like waves over the hillside rocks," says Miyano. ʻĀkia is a highly salt-tolerant plant native to Hawaiʻi.

The view from the kitchen extends over a seating area, along the pool, and beyond toward the Kona coastline. The waterfall edge at the end of the pool was designed to connect it visually to the ocean.

AN INFILTRATION OF ELEMENTS

When Franklin Marcus bought property with twenty miles of coastline as its view, his focus became creating a structure that merged in and out of the land around it.

"The landscape comes right into the house. At eleven hundred feet, it is high enough that certain winds will actually bring clouds through the house," says Marcus. "It only happens once or twice a year, but it's absolutely extraordinary when it does."

Volcanic rock formations rise up from slate floors to form a side table. An accidentally discovered lava tube serves as the wine cellar. Breezes from the upper reaches of Hualālai, one of the Big Island's three volcanoes, flow down the mountain through the house unfettered.

In order to preserve the *mauka makai*, or mountain-to-ocean breezes, every wall in this house is parallel. There are no perpendicular walls. On the mauka side there's nothing but louvers. Down on the makai side of the house, it's all sliding doors. It's a single stretch of space all the way across, so that air flow can be controlled in every room by opening and closing the windows and the doors.

"I really wanted Franklin to feel as if he was living outside: as close to the elements as was practical," says Boston architect Roel Krabbendam, who notes that he and Marcus designed the house with the concept of "flow" as its central theme.

185

Sliding doors allow the building's living room to open up to the outdoors as well as all the way through toward the master bedroom and its outdoor garden.

The home's entry was excavated out of the existing hillside. Stone steps lead across a koi pond into the core of the house. In the background, landscaping and hillside lava are integrated into the home's interior.

At the time, Krabbendam was working in public school design. Inspired by those industrial designs, he came up with the concept of the three central cores of parallel walls running all the way through the house.

"That structure solved a number of issues simultaneously," notes Krabbendam. "It gave us support for the roof, privacy between spaces, and complete penetration of breeze through the rooms. In the tropics, you need that unless you're going to rely on air conditioning. And the panel system allows Franklin to open or close the house as well as individual rooms as much as he likes."

Using the parallel walls, Krabbendam created modules of master bedroom and office, kitchen and living rooms, and then guest quarters. Lānai occupied the spaces between the modules once they were assembled together.

As the two men scribbled notes on their building plans, they identified areas of particular interest: the kitchen, the fireplace, and master bedroom. "Those focal points outlined in lopsided ellipses done in magic marker hung around long enough to become cones and planes that ultimately erupted out of the roof," says Krabbendam, referring to the massive skylights created on site for those areas, each of which is meant to echo the shape of a different Big Island volcano.

"We were going to create another skylight for the guest room, but it became too crowded and we felt we might take our theme too far. We'd taken as many elements of the outside as we could to infiltrate the house: running water in the entry, the lava, and the pool. At one point we tried running grass inside before practicality intervened."

"The master bedroom has a Japanese feeling to me," says Marcus. "I love the serenity of having an exterior shower and garden to one side and the view out toward the ocean to the front."

The master bedroom has the tall skylight reminiscent of Mauna Kea. The skylights were built on site, and this one was constructed at three separate angles to prevent bright light from hitting the bed.

The kitchen opens on one side to the pool and on another side to a private garden. Its skylight represents the Big Island volcano Mauna Loa. The mahogany wood used throughout the house was sourced in from a Costa Rican tree farm.

The home's entrance was designed by architect Roel Krabbendam as a "flying wing" that mirrors the home's roof line. The house is set amid Marcus' four-acre coffee farm.

Because of its smoothness, river rock collected from Big Island fields was used in the outdoor shower and wherever else in the home people might lean against it. The rougher a'a lava was used on exterior walls like the one to the left of the shower for its raw beauty.

"That issue of the pool shooting right out toward the ocean was a very big deal and no small commitment on Franklin's part," says Krabbendam. Running the pool close to the house and perpendicular to its current position would have been far less expensive. "Only a very strong commitment to the concept of flow and to the very visceral notion of swimming out to sea and the horizon made the present configuration conceivable."

But what was left was exactly as the two had originally imagined it. "Entering into this house feels more like immersing yourself into a very special environment than like stepping into a house," says Krabbendam. "Water, heat, stone, and breeze: it's a combination of the senses that makes you feel completely grounded."

Turkeys often come down from the mountainside to drink in the pool, which is pictured here at dusk. Twenty miles of the Kona coastline are visible from the house.